The Picaresque Element
in Western Literature

"It is only right, to my mind, that things so remarkable, which happen to have remained unheard and unseen until now, should be brought to the attention of many and not lie buried in the sepulcher of oblivion"

--Lazarillo de Tormes

Frederick Monteser

The Picaresque Element
in Western Literature

Studies in the Humanities No. 5

Literature

The University of Alabama Press
University, Alabama

To the memory of my father
WALTER RUDOLPH MONTESER
The finest scholar and gentleman I have ever known
This book is dedicated with deep love and sincere respect

Contents

Foreword

In considering the pícaro as both human being and literary genre, one must describe not only what he was, but also what he was not. The latter distinction may be even more important than the former.

The human race seemingly always includes the criminal in some form, and these asocial individuals are interesting and even exciting under suitably romantic conditions. They help to balance the scales of society by providing a counterweight to ostentatious virtue, and it is perhaps for this reason that they are tolerated. Among them we find the pícaro...

It is possible to identify pícaros in literature almost as soon as we can understand the literature itself. Obviously, then, the pícaro did not develop from the 16th century Spanish *novela*, but rather the reverse.

The purpose of this study is threefold: to examine the Picaresque Novel as a genre belonging to a particular social and historical epoch, to consider *Picarismo* as a continuing social phenomenon, and to attempt a prognosis for picaresque elements in future literature.

It is inevitable that so complex a character as the pícaro must engender widely divergent interpretations and identifications. No author can hold all of them simultaneously, and few would care to if it were possible. The first task faced is therefore a definition of those elements which are held in this study to be fundamental to *picarismo,* and an explanation of the opinion that others are inapplicable. This will be especially significant when one comes to consider Latin-American literature. The reader will be wise to remember, however, that it is an opinion which is being presented—there is no possibility of a consensus. If the reader is motivated to seek and identify pícaros in other works and countries, an important goal of the study will have been achieved, without regard to agreement with this or any other opinion.

One can never acknowledge all the help and suggestions which play a part in an investigation of this nature, but perhaps a small part of the debt may be defined—it cannot be repaid. My grateful appreciation is extended to Dr. Collice H. Portnoff, under whose guidance the study was originally begun many years ago. Dr. Brice Harris of Arizona State University gave most generously of his time and experience in guiding me, and read the manuscript with a benevolent harshness which was critical in the finest meaning of the term. I can never express adequately my debt to him, for teaching me the dignity of scholarship, and setting me an example to strive toward.

Dr. John Hamilton of the Foreign Languages department at Auburn University was most generous and helpful, and I am also deeply indebted to Mrs. Frances M. Honour, of the Ralph Brown Draughton Library, for her kind assistance on so many occasions. The author who has the guidance of Mr. James Travis, managing editor of the University of Alabama Press, is indeed fortunate, and to this gentleman I extend my thanks, not least for his very helpful suggestions in my research.

To my wife Harriet Lipp Monteser I offer, again, my deep gratitude for her endless patience and understanding when I made demands upon her as a typist and research assistant to which neither author nor professor is entitled, much less husband. Finally, my thanks go to Ginger, who never doubted me in the years during which I doubted myself.

To all of these I offer gladly a share in whatever good has come of our mutual effort—errors and shortcomings I reserve to myself alone.

                                                        FREDERICK MONTESER

1

The Pícaro: Who, When and Especially Why?

Of those elements which invigorate literature, none is so dependable as social disruption. Normalcy produces Babbits—one may sympathize with them, but seldom feels a strong emotional identification.

When the life of the individual is disrupted, however, situations of intense interest are generated by the sudden need for adjustment, and human beings in such situations are vital and significant. In other words, they form the basis of good stories.

Examples of this principle are legion, and a few selected at random should suffice to indicate the extent to which it is applicable.

Numerous works on the American Revolution exist, but among the most exciting is James Fenimore Cooper's *The Spy*. Yet it says less than, for example, St. Jean de Crèvecoeur's *Letters from an American Farmer*.

The reason for this is not difficult to ascertain. Harvey Birch is engaged in a fight for life and country, while the literate Frenchman concerns himself with "a good, honest plodding German Lutheran" who is doubtless worthy as a citizen but hardly impressive as a hero. This contrast may be equally evident in several works by a single author. Stephen Crane's Maggie is pitiable, but not even a rabid social critic would regard her as equal in interest to Henry Fleming in *The Red Badge of Courage*.

There is, in fact, a scale of interest which is positively correlated to the emotional intensity and danger to which the character (and therefore the empathetic reader) is exposed. One may, then, logically expect the most hostile environment to produce the most interesting personality.

Such a set of conditions undoubtedly existed in embryo in Spain toward the end of the 15th century, when conflict between the Cross and Crescent finally ended with a total capitulation of the Moors in Granada in 1492. Spain drew its first deep breath in seven hundred years, and looked about a little uneasily for something to do next.

Fortunately for both the multitude of soldiers of fortune, good and ill, and the peacefully inclined civilians who survived, the New World beckoned, and with a sigh of relief the battered watchers on the Iberian shore saw the adventurers sail away to confront the waiting lands to the west. Neither the direction nor the destination was really important to the surviving Spaniards—it was the departure that was so devoutly desired!

Having set afloat the tiger which had been held by the tail so gingerly and for so long, Spain was now blessed with a truly admirable monarch in the person of Charles I who, in 1516, donned the crown of Castile y León, which he later exchanged for that of the Holy Roman Empire. Both a humanist and Erasmist, Charles was a brilliant Empire builder, and it was only the disastrous wars of unification which changed what might have been an historically triumphant reign into a crushing prelude to the death of a nation's glory.

A well-unified, prosperous country might conceivably have endured the resultant outpouring of men and wealth, but Spain had never achieved complete economic development. The replacing of enterprising Moors and Jews with uneducated, unambitious peasants was fatal, not only to the arts but also to the productive trades which were the lifeblood of the country.

The aristocracy naturally gravitated to the Church, the court, or the army. Foreigners, willing to work hard and take a share of the little remaining wealth in circulation, flocked to the cities of Spain, while a native class of hopelessly, eternally and, worst of all, resignedly poor thieves and idlers developed.

It was in this world that the pícaro was born.

In sharp contrast to the not entirely defunct Spanish self-conception of *hidalgo,* that is, *un hijo de algo,* the pícaro by definition was so far from being "the son of someone" that he was often ignorant of his own parents.

Since such an unfortunate youth was inevitably a parasite, his stock in trade was his quick wits, which time and need sharpened to a razor edge. The stupid boy simply did not survive. The pícaro soon realized that honesty and faithfulness were luxuries which he could not afford, and his life proved the effectiveness with which he rid himself of such pernicious limitations. An Olympic runner may voluntarily carry handicap weights, but seldom an escaping Indian brave.

Chandler, in his encyclopedic *Literature of Roguery,* defines with considerable exactness the degree of criminality customary among, and permissible in the pícaro, before he assumes the full stature of villain or criminal:

> As the typical crime of the villain is murder, so the typical crime of the rogue is theft. To obliterate distinction of *meum* and *tuum* is the rogue's main business. He aspires to win by wit or dexterity what others have wrought by labor or received of fortune. He may cheat at cards or snatch purses. He may forge a check or a will. He may beg with a painted ulcer or float a commercial bubble. He may scheme for title and fortune by means of a worldly marriage, or pocket his hostess's spoons. He may prey on the government as a smuggler, illicit distiller, or counterfeit utterer. He may play the quack, levy blackmail, crack a safe, or even rob on the highway. But the use of personal violence usually ends his career as rogue and stamps him the villain. Thus the brigand and the pirate stand without the pale of roguery proper.[1]

The pícaro's mode of existence usually resulted in his exhausting his welcome in all but the largest towns in a minimum of time, and this process, repeated endlessly, resulted in the peripatetic life which was one of his characteristic traits.

His movements were normally in a horizontal social pattern, however, since his vital concern was survival, and he had little time indeed for romance or any ambition beyond a full belly.

A variation on this theme, not improbable in life, and artistically fascinating, is the pícara. Endowed by her sex with one commercially valuable resource denied to her male counterpart, it is obvious that the unfortunate girl early must have become involved in some degree of prostitution. Along with countless sordid real examples, with which history mercifully does not overburden us, the reader with room in his literary diet for a reasonable amount of erotic roughage will encounter the pícara in unmistakable form in both Fanny Hill[2] and Moll Flanders[3]. Even a Victorian suppression of the sexual motif does not invalidate the characterization, and Becky Sharp[4] is as entitled to her allegorical name as would be a full-blooded de Tormes.

There are a number of more or less typical characteristics of the true pícaro, which are often but not essentially made clear. For example, the pícaro is often a servant. A moment's reflection will show the reader that this is almost inevitable in an aristocratic society, for what is more logical than that a poor boy should become attached to a wealthy and powerful master? Again, this is possible but by no means essential to the characterization.

The pícara logically leaves in her wake a series of swindled and sometimes swindling lovers. The general structure of the personality still holds true, however, since the reader is constantly impressed with her desire to find a permanent husband and security. Survival continues to be paramount as, in realistic justice, it must.

Variations on the fundamental pícaro are endless, since each period in subsequent (and even preceding) literary history found a topicality to emphasize, which assumed an outsize aspect in the character as each saw it. Nevertheless, if one is to regard a work as truly related to this figure, it must be so delineated that both a real and apparent resemblance exist.

2

La Novela Picaresca:
Generic Form

While it might appear logical to assume that any work of long fiction which includes a pícaro is a picaresque novel, this is not true. The loose, sometimes almost undiscernible structure of the genre is often cited as an identifying formal element, but this is rather a symptom of the literature of the entire period, than of the picaresque novel per se.

There are, instead, other and more accurate criteria for defining the genre. To be sure, they must inevitably be subjective, and related more closely to the individual reader than to any universal concept, but subjectivity does not render them invalid. It means only that there is more than one "right" definition.

Frequency of occurrence is, of course, a logical basis for an inductive reasoning process, and it is perhaps the best method of approaching this particular problem. The following discussion will, accordingly, attempt to identify those characteristics and common denominators most typical of the orthodox picaresque literature.

To begin with, the pícaro must be the central character in his own story, even though it may not always be told from his "point of vision." One finds third person narrators, and a few isolated examples even use dialogue alone. The adventures of the pícaro are, however, always the motivating force and pivot of the principal action.

In fact, the tale of the pícaro's precarious adventures and existence may well be deemed the one essential aspect of a picaresque story, since the mere existence of a picaresque personality is not sufficiently unusual to place a work in that category.

It is by no means excessive to suggest that such a qualification is of greater importance than a strict adherence to the mechanical form of the genre. Form was, at best, a rather flexible matter in the literature of 16th century Spain, and the style and content were of much greater importance.

For this reason, it is quite proper to consider *La Celestina*[1] a legitimate predecessor of the picaresque novel, even though it is in the form of a play. Fernando de Rojas wrote it as a drama in sixteen, perhaps even twenty-one acts, but it was clearly intended as a "closet drama," not for production, and the result is more novel than play. The character of Celestina is clearly taken from Juan Ruiz's *Libro de Buen Amor*[2], and Lesley Byrd Simpson has acknowledged this interchange in genre by subtitling the work "A Novel in Dialogue."[3]

Any tale of the pícaro inevitably reflects unfavorably upon the environment in which it is placed, resulting in a satire on specific social conditions, especially *hidalguía,* but this is often a consequence rather than an intent. One should be careful to avoid this pitfall, since to remake a literature of entertainment into a sermon is to destroy its essential literary value and distort the author's intent.

The pícaro is concerned with survival in a hostile world, the author with telling a good tale, and usually neither is sociologically or didactically inclined. The picaresque novel developed in a society which could not but realize its own faults, with a beggar on every street corner. Why then would an author take the trouble to point out what everyone already knew? Chiefly to entertain, perhaps to ridicule, but certainly never to preach!

The charge of excessive didacticism is often leveled against the picaresque novel because of the long and often prosy sermons inserted among the thieves and beggars. This is a misinterpretation, or rather a lack of understanding of the pressures on the 16th century Spanish author. The light-hearted scribbler who took such obvious and vociferous delight in the immorality and dishonesty which characterized the pícaro would shortly find himself before a disapproving representative of the Inquisition, who was quite capable of declaring not only the book but the author as well to be a menace to public morals, and touching an ecclesiastically ignited match to both.

The ideal answer, obviously, was to write the story and placate the Church at the same time. Without changing the approach or concealing their tacit approval of the scamps about whom they wrote, authors found through experience the expedient of embodying distinct moral lectures in their tales, conveniently placed so that the reader might disregard them if he wished. In point of fact, perceptive readers did no such thing, since they often added to the satire by emphasizing the contrast between word and deed. Nevertheless, it is these *capatio benevolentiae* which are often mistaken for evidence of piety, which they are not.

This type of tongue-in-cheek virtue is exemplified in the incident of the exiled Moor.[4] This character devotes considerable breath and time to praising the laws which drove him from his country, while discussing his love for and loyalty to his former sovereign. The perceptive reader cannot but realize that the Moor's support of his king, in the face of unjust personal loss and exile, proves that he is a most desirable subject—far more so, in fact, than many of those who were permitted to remain. Cervantes seems to have been opposed to Philip's policy of expulsion, but many other authors dealt with the Church, the aristocracy, the professions and trades and almost every other source of traditional power in similar or equally effective ways. As Vincente Espinel, after reading *Guzmán de Alfarache,* commented with bitter approval to Mateo Alemán, "You put your finger on festering sores."

Another most interesting, if perhaps atypical, version of

the genre is the story involving transmigration of souls, which is presented in several notable works. One in particular duplicates the movement of a servant from one master to another by substituting the changing of a soul from one body to another.[5] This type of conceit must, however, be regarded as essentially a ramification and not the main branch. In fact, although the picaresque novel may on occasion have a somewhat fantastic aspect, the very nature of the subject demands a comparatively realistic treatment. It is difficult to be very ambiguous about starvation!

It may be claimed that the picaresque novel was actually the historic counterpart of the European novel of manners, although it is improbable that Henry James would be eager to acknowledge this artistic ancestry for his writings. Dealing primarily with behavior and relationships, rather than events, such authors as Mateo Alemán attempted to present a picture of what it was like to live in the period, rather than what others did in it. The result has been described with admirable clarity as "the comic biography (or more often the autobiography) of an anti-hero."[6]

This approach produced a natural emphasis on social satire, and leads with startling directness to the works of Ben Jonson, Shakespeare and (if this be not blasphemy) even Jane Austen. Much in drama and long fiction deals with the less-than-acceptable social character, but the picaresque novel was the first European genre to identify so completely with the anti-hero.

The general attitude of the picaresque novel was surprisingly democratic in nature, and the viewpoint of the aristocrat was almost never considered. Spain had experienced so much of the non-productive aristocratic philosophy of life, including a complete disregard of the utter impoverishment of so many commoners, that hardship among the titled was regarded rather as poetic justice than a matter for concern. We touch upon possibly *simpático* points of the nobility briefly in Lazarillo's tenure with the impoverished young squire. "I could see that he didn't own a thing and couldn't have done any better. I was more inclined to pity him than to resent him." Nevertheless, the best that Lazarillo can do is to be sorry, which is a long way from respect.

There was a wide difference in the personal attitudes of authors toward the society in which their respective pícaros lived, which is apparent more in style than in actual incident.

The genial, kindly Cervantes, with a genuine love for humanity, is at the upper end of the scale—while he was often satirical, he was never bitter or cynical. In his *Novelas Ejemplares* (1613), especially *Rinconete y Cortadillo* in which he deals in some detail with the underworld of Seville, there is much that is critical and even sordid, as there must have been in 17th century Spain, but the descriptions are sympathetic and sorrowing and the criticism restrained.

Quevedo, on the other hand, made no effort to conceal his cynical attitude toward his fellow man, and much of his work is not only realistic and probably true, but gives an impression of bitterness and cruelty.[7] This is not to say that the work is unjust or unskillful—it is cleverly constructed and contains a wealth of incident and good characterization, of which Cabra is not the least famous example.

Regardless of the author or his attitude toward society, the pícaro himself is usually the only character who stays before the reader during the entire story, and in whose destiny the reader is expected to stay interested. In his peripatetic career the pícaro encounters as many other personalities as the author's ingenuity (or possibly his supply of ink) permits, but it is only in their relationship to the central character that they have significance. In fact, Chandler takes this as his central point of definition, by stating "When the rogue and his tricks constitute the main source of interest, the novel in which he figures is a picaresque novel."[8]

3

Pícaro vs.

Picaresque

The preceding chapters have implied that there is a specific set of characteristics which may be labeled picaresque, and that there are distinct limits to its scope. It is therefore germane to examine the content and characteristics of *Picarismo* in an effort to assist identification in other eras and genres.

The question is, of course, highly subjective and one of personal identification. None of the authors of the Golden Age concerned himself with an academic definition of his own or anyone else's work, and one is therefore faced with the problem of imposing a 20th century frame upon a 17th century picture.

The danger of this procedure is an almost-inevitable assumption that human values in the Spain of Quevedo, de Rojas, and Cervantes were those of modern America, and the result has been that much learned discussion has been quite pointless. To speculate and, what is worse, draw conclusions when an author himself did not consider a particular facet of his own literary creation is really a re-creation of the character, rather than an analysis. Since there is no real evidence to consider, the best that can result is clever psychological guesswork, and no means for determining whether it is right or wrong.

A case in point is Robert Alter's extensive digression into Lazarillo's Christianity,[1] which rather resembles Shakespeare's seacoast of Bohemia: the reader is told that it exists, but nothing more. Lazarillo was born of a Christian mother, in a Christian country, and there the matter quite literally ends. To assume, as a few critics have done, that every mention of God, angels, or the Holy Ghost is evidence of Christian feeling is utterly fallacious. Spaniards, and especially those of earlier centuries, are often quite casual in their mention of religious matters which, to a modern Anglo-Saxon speaker of English, require formal circumstances such as a sermon, to avoid the suggestion of blasphemy. Neither respect nor disrespect is necessarily involved—only habit.

In *Lazarillo de Tormes,* however, it was the author's clear intent to pour scorn upon the Church and everything connected with it, ending with the ultimate sneer of marrying the boy to a priest's mistress. Is it likely that he would have made Lazarillo much interested in respecting his own or any other religion?

To attempt to go beyond the actual statements and events of a picaresque story, and to impose upon it critical theory and erudition which contribute neither to an understanding of *picarismo* nor to the explication of a specific work, is a pitfall which this work will try to avoid. It is, in all fairness, a most tempting type of academic exercise, but quite unjustified in a work based primarily upon ascertainable facts.

In attempting to codify a set of specific characteristics for the pícaro himself, and obviously they must be equally applicable to a female if the definition is to be valid, economic level is perhaps the best starting point. From Lazarillo forward, the eternal problem of survival in a hostile society seems to have claimed most of the pícaro's attention, as indeed it must. In fact, almost every Spanish commoner's primary concern in the 16th century was with finding enough to eat. To realize this one need only note that the first three *tratados* of Lazarillo's tale deal primarily with matters of food and hunger, and that his parents' downfall, his birth, and his expulsion from his home into the world are all the result of a need for food.

There is, however, a somewhat modifying factor which should be considered in placing this admittedly fundamental motivation in proportion, since it was not the only need involved. Gerald Brennan comments with considerable perception that all Spanish writing "is the literature of a people who have scarcely ever known security or comfort,"2 and this is just my point. It was not a temporary nor a traumatic matter, but rather a basic aspect of life in 16th century Spain.

There is little starvation among English-speaking occidentals in our time, and the concept, rather like leprosy and smallpox (both of which are very much still in existence), appears to us as something horrible and unreal. To ask an over-fed American suburbanite to believe that hunger was as much a part of a Spanish pícaro's life as advertising is in America is to ask a great deal—perhaps too much.

Nevertheless, this realization is one without which the picaresque novel may well be meaningless. If one sees the pícaro as being only mildly concerned with food, his "suspension of disbelief," no matter how willing, cannot suffice to justify actions which would be inexplicable in any other situation. For example, Lazarillo's involved machinations with the priest's bread chest3 would be ridiculous in view of the few crumbs which result, if it were not that those crumbs were literally necessary to him to sustain life.

It is perhaps unfair to misuse a work of entertainment as a textbook in economics, but it is nevertheless true, as René Wellek points out, that "used as a social document, literature can be made to yield the outlines of social history."4 It is equally true that some understanding of social history is necessary as a prerequisite to an understanding of literature.

There is one outstanding exception to the resigned acceptance of hunger as a normal aspect of living, and that is in *Guzmán de Alfarache*. While Guzmán is, in most other respects, a normal enough pícaro, there is a single unique item in the story, and that is the emphasis placed upon the distortion of the personality by the demands of hunger.

Mateo Alemán's pícaro is bitterly pessimistic, and resentful in a way not apparently true of other pícaros. Hunger is *not* accepted by Guzmán but rather is consciously regarded as a symbol of the pain which is part of man's price for survival in a hostile world. It would appear, however, that although hunger is always present it is almost never predominant. The need to realize this is especially apparent when one realizes that the hungry pícaro, at least in literature, did not starve. Hunger satisfied, the pícaro still had other problems, and they too form an essential part of his life and adventures.

The Spanish pícaro was usually a member of the lower classes in origin, although occasionally one finds that he has fallen from a presumably higher estate. Whether it is his original poverty or his laziness which has caused his present condition, his adventures require that he be both destitute and absolutely without resources other than his wits.

The etymology of the most fundamental term in a book is surely of significance, including its history, and so the word *pícaro* is worthy of some consideration. It is, surprisingly, quite indefinite in its meaning, even to a Spaniard, but I must take exception to an all too common belief that pícaro appeared for the first time in Spain in the middle of the 16th century, in *Guzmán de Alfarache* by Mateo Alemán.

Ernest Mérimée has dealt with this question in his encyclopedic discussion, and his statement appears the most authoritative. According to him, *pícaro* was first used in 1548, when it appeared in the *Carta del Bachiller de Arcadia al Capitan Salazar.*[5] The word is not found in *Lazarillo*, and appears restricted to Spanish works. There is no direct translation in any other language, and *narquoise, larron* and *schelm* all fall short in connotation. Substitution is equally unsatisfactory. Robert Alter, for example, uses *picaroon* as the means of identifying Moll Flanders as a female picaresque personality, which simply cannot be justified.[6] The word for a female pícaro is obviously *pícara, picaroon* is a male, and the result is confusion.

There has been a good deal of scholarly speculation about the etymology and meanings of the term *picaro*, a few of which are here presented:

1. *Picado*—pitted with small-pox.
2. *Picardy*—the province where Spaniards saw ragged, dirty characters in the time of Carlos V.
3. *Pico*—sharp.
4. *Picante*—sharp or biting.
5. *Picar (Pinchar)*—to pinch.

Dictionaries are of little assistance in this regard, since Velásquez offers "knavish, roguish, vile, low, mischievous, malicious, crafty, sly, merry, gay, loafer,"[7] to which one can only reply "No doubt" and go on from there.

Webster settles upon the word "rogue,"[8] admittedly the most common English translation, but then selects the Picardy background as the correct origin, a commitment of dubious wisdom.

It is a serious blunder to assume that picaresque literature is restricted to the basic problems and adventures of a picaro. It is far more than this, and as a result the reader is occasionally confronted with a work of almost no definable classification, which is nevertheless quite clearly picaresque.

The picaresque novel has been described as "psychology without entrails,"[9] and there is some basis for this attitude. Nevertheless, a sort of inhuman efficiency in living is not the only thing offered the reader. There is the picaro's world per se, and one function of the novel was clearly to contrast the society pictured with that microcosm which is the picaro.

It has been suggested that one of the major functions of the picaresque novel is to reflect the social conditions as they impinge upon the central personality. It is quite true that the fundamental Spanish picaro occurred at the point of incipient deterioration in that nation's history, but this does not necessarily postulate that *picarismo* can exist only at such a point in an historical cycle. The picaresque novel was not a unified genre, nor was it a stationary form. To say that a single aspect remained true for its entire history (which is by no means ended yet, as this study will attempt to show) is debatable, since such a qualification has the inevitable effect of slicing a literary continuum into bite-sized books. Instead one may, with a little imagination, trace the progress of the genre from Lazarillo to last Sunday's book reviews.

The early picaresque literature, such as *La Celestina,* was both realistic and idealistic, in that it combined the very basic problems of life ("If you want to get something done you've got to pay for it.") with such flights of fancy as "Love is the enemy of all reason and gives its gifts to those who serve it least." The story was the point, however, and the poetic moments are comparatively few and unemphasized.

Satire was almost always present, whether the target was Lazarillo's beggar: "It was mostly inn-wives, barmaids, candy sellers, whores and other little women like that that he prayed for. He hardly ever offered up a prayer for a man... Young as I was, I was struck by the blind man's discretion and prudence..." or Cervantes: "I am not adapted to palace life, for I have a sense of shame and am not good at flattery."

There was a certain reluctance upon the part of Cervantes, however, which one does not find in those bitter denouncements of society which Quevedo so enjoyed. The latter took delight in such comments as the description in *La Vida del Buscón* of Cabra, the miserly schoolmaster whose "eyes, stuck close together in his head seemed to be peering out through wicker baskets, and were so sunk and shady that they would have been a good place for a market stall." Cervantes, on the other hand, seemed to regret the inevitability of criticism, and his canine philosopher Berganza admits regretfully, "wrongdoing and the speaking of evil are something that we inherit from our forebears and drink in with our mother's milk."

Cervantes was the exception, however, and the picaresque novel in Spain was, generally speaking, one long verbal castigation of society, subject only to the limiting influence of the Inquisition. The result has been a very natural assumption that the purpose of the genre is social criticism, which is not entirely true. While such authors as Quevedo and Fernando de Rojas saw much to criticize, and were glad to be heard on the subject of social failings, their essential purpose remained that of the storyteller, and if one is to seek to identify the pícaro in other eras that elusive youth should be regarded as a person—not a moral tract!

The best evidence to support this opinion is the simple fact that many picaresque novels are autobiographical, as Werner P. Friedrich points out, since they are told in the first person by the boy or ex-boy whose adventures are to be revealed:

> It often happened that the detailed account of how these gutter-born urchins worked their way up through a corrupt society until they themselves achieved some semblance of power or respectability and a hard-boiled philosophy of life tended to approach the level of personal memoirs and autobiographies on the part of the author.[10]

Much is to the pícaro's discredit, some fatally so from a moral point of view, and what remains to the reader is often neither edifying nor improving, but simply highly entertaining.

Perhaps even the greater portion write as older men, about their youthful adventures. Given the situation of a naïve youth wrestling endlessly with the problems of survival in a severely materialistic world, the Spanish flavor which results in the stories is uniquely bitter-sweet. There is an additional delight to the pícaro, since he is usually speaking now as a virtuous, reformed citizen, and can therefore admit unabashedly the frolics and tricks of his youth. Elisha Kane sums up this effect succinctly when he comments, "In [the] strange contrasting character of Spanish letters lies much of its strength."

A hard, bitter realism is nevertheless to be found in any picaresque work, together with a naturalism which thrives upon the ugly and cruel. Deaths such as those of Sempronio and Parmento ("One was senseless, with his brains running out, and the other had both his arms broken and his face smashed.") and Calisto ("Gather up our luckless master's brains from the stones and put them back in his skull.") are common, and the pícaro is seldom shocked by them.

This is, of course, indicative of the fact that there is little dignity left to characters in a picaresque novel, the hero or anyone else. Even death is not allowed to be solemn, and is either brutalized or laughed at. Propriety is a fault to which the human race is over-addicted, according to the pícaro, and he delights in puncturing bubbles of self-righteousness. Whether one died in a silk and ebony fourposter, surrounded by bishops and grieving family, or was drowned in a sewer, the result is equally final and this is all that interested the pícaro. His business was to stay alive, and he left honor to those who had the leisure to pursue it. The pícaro was usually a servant or beggar, and honor to him was a reflection, not an emanation. *El Licenciado Vidriera* puts this sentiment neatly when the madman points out: "The honor of the servant depends upon that of the master; and so just look and see whom it is you serve, and you will see how much honor you possess."

The sexual problem, although subordinate to that of hunger, is often present and there is little reticence about it. Mother Celestina makes no bones about being a procuress, Justina is an out-and-out whore, and Lazarillo de Tormes ends his days married to the priest's mistress. The contrast between the high flights of poetry about love and the simple fact of sexual intercourse form a satirical contrast which is one of the strongest of all picaresque effects.

Since the purpose of this study is an effort to identify pícaros and picaresque elements in works of other epochs and countries, it seems necessary to attempt a codification of the picaresque elements which have been discussed above, which can then be used as a criterion for further discussion:

1. The pícaro must be an individual of comparative youth, presently in great poverty, who has no financial or

professional resources to which he may reasonably look for
security. If he can, by swallowing his pride, escape from his
present circumstances and become socially acceptable, he is
not a pícaro.

Phrased differently, *picarismo* is never voluntary, and
therefore does not result from deliberate adventures.

2. The pícaro must restrict his activities to minor criminal
acts, refraining from deliberate violence for its own sake, and
foregoing murder or pointless evil.

An animal in a jungle does not go about killing aimlessly,
unless he is rabid. The analogy is valid, since the pícaro, like
the predator, seeks only survival, and pointless violence on
his part could result only from insanity.

3. The pícaro must be conscious, either during his
adventures or later as a mature author, of the reflections
upon society which his tale points up. He need not criticize
but he must be aware of what the reader is to criticize.

The bitter strength of a picaresque tale is, in fact, frequently created by the protagonist's apparent naïveté as he
related disgusting or disgraceful events with no apparent understanding of their significance. The insistence that the
reader draw his own conclusions is a form of involvement
which an author like Cervantes or Fernández de Lizardi used
frequently and with great skill.

4. The pícara, inevitably a whore, may exhibit an earthy
pleasure in sex, but the story must show that her moral situation is the result of social helplessness, not promiscuity.
Along with her male counterpart, she is just trying to survive,
and would much rather use legitimate means if they were
available to her.

Moll, Fanny, Trutz, and the rest all declare again and again
that they seek only security, and prove it by withdrawing
completely from their former activities when the occasion
presents itself.

5. The work of literature, to be picaresque, must include a
discussion of the basic problem of physical survival in a realistic, practical manner.

It is this criterion which clearly and finally excludes from consideration all of the large fraternity of policemen, detectives, amateurs in crime, and assorted thrill-seekers. To suggest that a person whose life includes a respectable occupation, a home and family, and future security is a pícaro is to broaden the scope of the genre to a point at which it is merely meaningless.

If the protagonist's basic need is not sheer survival, he is not a pícaro!

6. The world of the picaresque story must be an unsympathetic one, not necessarily to everyone, but definitely to the pícaro. He must be so placed as to be forced to compete with others of greater strength and advantages, so that the odds of his winning are always against him.

If the pícaro is overtly on the side of law and order, if he works against crime by assisting the police, or if his avocation is either crime or crime-detection, he is actually supporting and supported by the world in which he lives, and thereby contradicts this essential portion of his rôle.

As one departs from the *Siglo de Oro,* the variations on the picaresque begin to move further and further from this rather rigid definition, but the fundamental aspects remain identifiable. While Captain Blood is too much of the adventurer, Lovelace too wealthy, and Maggie too ineffectual, there are nevertheless many literary figures which both precede and succeed Lazarillo, yet share some of his basic problems and attributes.

The 20th century, in particular, will offer that unique version of the pícaro designated the "anti-hero." The problem to be considered in its proper chronological position is that the pícaro had a habit of winning his battle, and the anti-hero's end is often a matter of intense psychological controversy.

Before beginning to explore literary indebtedness to the generic Spanish stories, however, it may be well to consider to what they themselves looked for example and model.

4

The Original

Spanish Literature

To begin with, this writer adopts the most usual position by holding that the first true Spanish Picaresque Novel was *La Vida de Lazarillo de Tormes.* Without this basis of understanding, much cannot be dated relatively.

It is quite true that this tale was preceded chronologically some twenty-four years by the *Retrato de la Lozana Andaluzana,* based upon an exposé of Roman customs during the Renaissance. While this work has the distinction of creating the first Spanish anti-heroine, the Andalusian Francisco Delicado was concerned with a vehicle for criticism, and not the telling of a story.

The Cabazuela village priest sets his story in Italy, not Spain, and it is raw, often amusing, but only by coincidence picaresque. It is really the tale of a roving whore, which is hardly the same thing as a pícara.

If one accepts this distinction between pícara and prostitute, and there is almost no reason to deny it, he has the advantage of the definite beginning data of 1554, when *Lazarillo* was published initially and simultaneously in Antwerp, Burgos, and Alcalá de Henares. There is a strong suggestion that there may have been a 1553 Antwerp edition, but since none has ever been discovered, or even established beyond doubt, it is customary to accept the 1554 statement.

With his usual prompt interest in such matters, the General

Inquisitor Valdés placed the book on the *Index* in 1559, presumably because of the priest and the seller of indulgences in the story. Nevertheless, Philip II caused an expurgated version to be printed in Madrid in 1573, which was followed by at least four known reprintings.

There is a great deal of scholarly and popular speculation regarding the author of this work, which can all be summed up by saying simply, "We don't know."

The only reasonable assumption, based upon solid internal evidence, is that it was not an unlettered pícaro who was the author of the tale. The studied simplicity of the style, the skillful depiction of types, and the references to classical myths, Pliny, Marcus Tullius, Galen, and Alexander surely point to an educated and perhaps cultured source. In that age, such a formidable literary repertoire might have been possessed by any modestly placed student, but it could not possibly have been Lazarillo himself.

It is not surprising that there was a second part to *Lazarillo* published a year later, but this was a spurious sequel and, except for verbal repetition of the last words of the first part, unrelated to it. In fact, it is so far removed in spirit as to be worth no consideration as a picaresque novel.

There was actually an hiatus of almost half a century before the next genuine success. This was the first portion of Mateo Alemán's *Primera Parte de la Vida de Guzmán de Alfarache,* which appeared in 1599.

There are two significant points which must be considered in placing this work in the perspective of the genre. First, this was a much larger plan, deliberately complicated and carefully designed in the manner of the modern novel, instead of merely a pleasant sketch of a few amusing adventures.

Perhaps even more important is that the second half of the sixteenth century was as different from the preceding years as sour grapes from wine. Charles V was gone, and now the dour Philip II slumped despondently upon an impoverished throne, with the understandable result that the Hispanic

world was disillusioned and dispirited, including the once-gay
pícaro.

Guzmán himself is disagreeable and sullen, and it is only
his being first condemned to the galleys for life and then set
free which directs him to a more socially acceptable life.

The book promises a sequel, and in 1603 a Valencian, Juan
Martí, tried to profit by an unauthorized fulfillment of
Alemán's promise. Not only was the book unsuccessful, but
in 1605 Alemán took his revenge by publishing what was
unmistakably the real sequel, by the real author, and including among the rogues the imposter Martí. The thought
that Pope might have been thinking of this at the time of *The
Dunciad* is irresistible!

It is worth noting that Alemán took his personal pícaro
beyond the borders of Spain, into Italy, which may well have
reflected the *Retrato de la Lozana Andaluzana* and led the
parade of such international heroes (or anti-heroes) in other
countries which was to follow shortly.

The Spanish ancestress of Moll Flanders appeared on the
scene at about this point when, in 1603, a Toledo physician
named Francisco de Ubeda published his *Pícara Justina*. Describing possibly the first avowed anti-heroine, after the
Lozana Andaluzana, it established the female counterpart of
Lazarillo for many generations to come.

It is quite possible to catalogue a great number of such
attempts of lesser stature, dealing with both sexes, but the
next major effort was by Juan de Luna, a Spaniard living in
Paris. In 1620 he issued a "corrected version" of *Lazarillo*
which almost matches the original in technique and interest,
if not in realism. It serves to illustrate the progress of the
genre, however, in its comparatively strong emphasis on the
pícaro per se, as opposed to his physical adventures.

A work which is worthy of a particular position appeared
in 1626, when Francisco de Quevedo y Villegas, of Zaragoza,
published his *História de la vida del Buscon llamado don
Pablos*. Ranging over such varied aspects of Spanish life as

universities, prisons, actors and the unforgettable Cabra, keeper of the student's boarding house at Salamanca, the cruel satire pictures life with all of Quevedo's cynical perception. The matrimonial cheats are unforgettable as well, and are equalled only by the "Sueños," published at about the same period, which deal with approximately the same material.

Miguel de Cervantes Saavedra entered the lists in 1613 with the *Novelas Ejemplares* and by creating the memorable Ginés de Pasamonte, who he declared would exceed Lazarillo's adventures, if the story were ever written. It is our eternal loss that this tale was never told.

The twelve *Novelas Ejemplares* themselves seem to have been Cervantes' way of proving that he was not unduly influenced by the forbidden Italian examples, such as that of Boccaccio. The word *novela* at this time signified a short story, rather than a novel in the modern sense, and this is what the *Novelas Ejemplares* really are.

Although there has been much scholarly attribution of Cervantes' work to such models as Apuleius and Lucian, this indebtedness is clearly not necessary, since the Spaniard might well have ignored them and still have been great.

Especially interesting in this group of tales is *Rinconete y Cortadillo,* since it reveals Cervantes' profound and not altogether explicable knowledge of *germanía,* the thieves jargon of Seville in which the story is placed.

Cervantes' greatest work was, of course, *Don Quijote,* but the picaresqueness of this story is open to debate. There is a certain subtle but still definitely rosy haze in which the good knight and his Sancho move, which seems to deny the necessary element of realism, the desperate struggle which one finds in *Lazarillo* or *Pícara Justina. Don Quijote* can almost be said to constitute a genre by itself, and that genre is not the picaresque.

The orthodox genre continued to bloom with increasing brilliance, and with an ever-wider spreading of the petals.

Vincente Espinel took his *Marcos de Obregonnot* not only to Italy, but to Algiers as well. In *Desordenada Codicia de los Bienes Angenos* Dr. Carlos García dealt with the tricks and arts of professional Spanish rogues, and more especially with their several grades and levels.

By now the pícaro was treading the boards as well in a number of plays such as *El Sagáz Marido Examinado* by Alonso Gerónima de Salas Barbadillo.

An interesting reversion to the original type was *La Vida y Hechos de Estevamollo Gonzales,* written in 1646, in which the adventures of a rascally buffoon are related in the true Lazarillo manner.

Perhaps the final effort in the true genre was *Periquillo, él de las Gallineras,* published in 1668. With the death at the end of the book of this pícaro-turned-philosopher, Spain bade farewell to the pícaro. Juan de Zavaleta[1] dealt not with a pícaro but rather with a villain, and the spell was at an end.

The former pícaro turned to murder, piracy, wit, and philosophy, and while he might still have been the source of a good tale, he was no longer Lazarillo. He did not live (and die) in Spanish literature alone, however, and he, or at least his Gallic blood-brother, can be found in another country of Europe at that period.

5

Pícaro

au Français

Although the pícaro had begun his long career in Spanish literature by a little after the middle of the sixteenth century, and French printers were responsible for many original Spanish publications, it was not until 1596 that there was any evidence of creative Gallic interest in the genre.

In this year an unknown author published *La Vie Genereuse des Mercelots, Gueuz, et Boesmiens.* There is no doubt that he can claim membership among the Iberian charter members, but the actual format of the tale is quite different. In the French approach, a nine year old boy runs away and joins a series of groups of vagabonds, eventually finding a band of gypsies. With them he attends a convention of rogues from all over France, and the reader is thus presented with a detailed description of their language, actions, tricks, etc. Different, perhaps, but nevertheless clearly a picaresque tale in the original design.

There appears to have been a preoccupation with the thieves' and rogue's language, for one finds *Le Jargon, ou le Langage de l'Argot Reformé,* and shortly thereafter *Réponse et Complaincte au Grant Coesre sur le Jargon de l'Argot Reformé.*

The helpless pícaro was made a vehicle for political argument, as well as etymological research, and a sort of nocturnal thieves congress on the Pont Neuf appears in

Reigles, Statuts, et Ordonnances de la Caballe des Filous.
Their own affairs settled, in 1607 they were then pictured, at
least those who were beggars, as debating government
reforms in *Chimaere seu Phantasma Mendicorum.*

The Spanish influence at this point is extremely doubtful—
gratifying so—since one would hate to assign such grave
public conscience to Lazarillo and his contemporaries.

It is nevertheless true that the standard Spanish picaresque
works had been translated into French, and were undoubtedly beginning to be reflected by the northern peoples
in their lighter literature. *Lazarillo* had been available in
French translation since 1561, although it had not yet
achieved the stature in France that distinguished the story in
its native country, and *Guzmán de Alfarache*[1] was translated
and published in 1600. From then on the trend was almost a
snowballing in its gathering momentum.

Don Quijote and the *Novelas Ejemplares* crossed the
Pyrenees in 1618, the *Engaños deste Siglo* and *Marcos de
Obregón* followed, and La Geneste finished Quevedo's
Sueños and *Buscón* in 1633. The interest in the latter con-
tinued for many decades, and one finds Raclot's translation
in 1699 and that of Restif de la Bretonne in 1766.[2] With
Gallic delicacy, *La Pícara Justina* became *La Narquoise
Justine* in 1635, and in 1661 *Garduña* was offered as *La
Fouyne de Seville.*

Several notable works such as the *Euphormionis Lusinini
Satyricon* (which was as much dependent upon the classics as
upon the Iberian Peninsula), *Argenis* and the *Avantures du
Baron de Faeneste* prepared the way for the coming of the
true pícaro, but he did not actually arrive until Charles Sorel
published *La Vrye Histoire Comique de Francion* in 1622.

In that year the first of the three installments was released
and, the first of twelve books, was an immediate and great
success. Less concerned with the comparatively crude realism
which had preceded it, the book dealt with all levels of
society, and concerned itself with individuals rather than
social groups.

A major difference was that the anti-hero was no longer a servant but rather the scion of nobility, a gallant adventurer, and a most enthusiastic exponent of eroticism. This was an element which affected the entire future of the genre in France, and which was responsible for a degree of maturity and interest in the picaresque hero which could not have existed among the comparatively juvenile Spanish protagonists.

It is a prominent motif in the *Histoire Générale des Larrons,* that loose but fascinating collection of almost seventy case histories which later served so many authors for source material. (Once in awhile they even admitted it...)

The leading author of this new school was Paul Scarron, who combined admittedly borrowed tales with so novel a method of presentation that he continued to exert a distinct literary influence even on the novels of the eighteenth century.

The compass needle continued to swing back and forth across that true north originally established by *Lazarillo*: then in 1662 it locked briefly but accurately upon the *Avantures Tragicomiques du Chevalier de la Gaillardise.* César Oudin de Préfontaine held closely to the Spanish model, but either due to a lack of literary value, or perhaps because of what has just been suggested as a merit, the story of the unfortunate orphan never achieved the popularity of many others of the period.

A burlesque trend next appeared with Charles d'Assoucy and his notable autobiography.[3] His page, Pierrotin, is more than a little reminiscent of Lazarillo, but the story itself is quite different.

Scarron continued to hold his position in French letters, despite this side branching. He persisted in placing his scenes in France, usually around Le Mans, but the inspiration was surely Spanish when he sat down to produce the *Roman Comique* in 1651.

The Spanish playwrights were exerting a major influence upon such noteworthy drama as was being produced in

France, and Scarron, Corneille and others drew upon this indirect source as well. This effect was brief, however, and the full impact is not to be felt until Le Sage appears.

In 1708 the experiment in burlesque had ended, and satire was again firmly established. Now the church became the target of one barbed pen after another. The Abbé Oliver had no sooner finished *L'infortuné Napolitain ou les Avantures du Seigneur Rozelli* than one finds *Les Libertins en Campagne* and *Les Tours de Maître Gonin,* surely an overwhelming barrage when one considers that the total span is only five years!

Sufficient spleen having been vented upon the not-unsoiled Cloth of the day, realistic adventure became the new direction of fiction in France, and the pre-Dumas *Mémoires de M. d'Artagnan* in 1700 was typical of the type. It is quite true that *Les Trois Mousquétaires* is far more enduring than Gatien Courtilz de Sandras' version, but the fact remains that this dashing soldier and his rascally companion Besmaux were the picaresque origin of a much ennobled and refined successor.

A number of others followed in the now well-trod path, including the *Mémoires du Chevalier du Compte de Gramont* in 1713, but it was the Scotsman Anthony Hamilton, the partner-in-exile of Charles II of France, who produced the inimitable *Mémoires du Chevalier Hassard,* in which the pícaro rose from his rags and pilfering to join Mazarin and Louis XIV in what was, at least, a more impressive variety of trickery.

It was in 1715, however, with Alain-René Le Sage at the height of his powers, that *Gil Blas* was produced and with it the perfection of the pícaro in France. Following the tradition of the anti-hero in service, his satirical exposé of the manners and customs of the day and the progress from poverty to plenty, Le Sage observed the established format. In selecting his pícaro from middle-class respectability, however, and endowing him with a conscience, Le Sage re-directed the emphasis of the genre toward a more general criticism of human failings, instead of the specific personalities and professions which had characterized Lazarillo and his blood brothers.

Le Sage made numerous other contributions to the picaresque novel such as the *Avantures de M. Robert Chevalier, dit de Beauchêne* (1732), in which the anti-hero prowls the world seeking and escaping from adventures; *Bachelier de Salamanque* (1736), in which Mexican life was pictured; and the *Histoire d'Estevanille Gonzalés,* which almost literally shreds the Inquisition. In addition to these Le Sage was directly responsible for a number of excellent translations of Spanish works.

The list of his own original works is endless. They eventually found admirers to translate them into German, English, Italian and even, by one Abate Alcino, a translation of *Gil Blas* into purest Castilian with the comment that it was a "work restored to its original idiom." That this may have been morally true does not alter the fact that the work in question was of the most unquestionably French origin.

Gil Blas, it must sadly be acknowledged, was the peak, and from it there was only decline. The genre in France, for many generations of writers to come, was to serve as a springboard until eventually there was a great and enduring revival in Hugo and Balzac.

6

The Germanic

Pícaro

In considering Germanic associations with the pícaro, one must acknowledge clear beginnings before *Lazarillo de Tormes*—in fact, as much as three hundred years earlier.[1] Since there will presently be a consideration of earlier periods in a separate chapter, this may be set aside for the moment in order to deal with the contemporary flowerings of this rather bitter-sweet plant.

The sixteenth century "jest-book" was the basis for the Teutonic version of the pícaro, but its effect was superficial. The effective origin was the *Liber Vagatorum*, which appeared in 1510. In it, along with a *Rothwelsch* vocabulary, was an account of some thirty mendicant orders, drawn from such sources as the criminal trials at Basel. The effects of, and indebtedness to, this work are almost endless.

In 1517 Pamphilus Gengenbach converted it into verse, Martin Luther turned it back to prose in 1528, and Giacinto Nobili used it as the basis for his *Vagabondo* in 1627. This last was translated into French in 1644, and so it went, on and on. It is to be found even in the first English beggar books, such as Awdeley's *Fraternitye of Vacabondes* and Harman's *Caveat for Common Cursitors.*

In addition to literary indebtedness, there are many translations, although most were accomplished with considerably more enthusiasm than accuracy. *Guzmán de Alfarache* was more or less translated in 1615 by Aegidius Albertinus, with additional German, Swiss and French incidents. *Celestina* became available in German in 1620 and in Latin in 1624, due to the efforts of Kasper Barth. Martin Freudenhold originated a sequel to *Guzmán de Alfarache,* composed of Eastern adventures, and Niclas Ulenhart translated both *Lazarillo de Tormes* and *Rinconete y Cortadillo.*

An outstanding exponent of the Spanish works was Georg Philipp Harsdörffer, who used several of the classical stories in the *Frauenzimmer Gesprächspiele,* as well as translating Cervantes.

The Thirty Years War stirred up a hornet's nest of satire, producing such biting comments as Hans Michael Moscherosch's *Gesichte Philanders von Sittewald* in 1639, and inspiring that outstanding German explicator of roguery, Hans Jakob Christoffel von Grimmelshausen. It is in his *Der Abentheurliche Simplicissimus* that one finds the first German novel of manners.

The German pícaro almost always became involved somehow with the military, a reflection of both *Zeitgeist* and *Volkgeist.* This holds true not only for the males, but for the Amazons as well, of whom Courage and Trutz Simplex are fair examples. I suggest that the last especially may have been Defoe's model for Moll Flanders.

Although it appears that *Trutz Simplex* was probably based by von Grimmelshausen upon the classic *Pícara Justina,* with possibly a touch of the French version which he may well have known as *La Narquoise Justine* (1635), it is worth noting that their English sister Moll is described by Defoe on the original title page of his work as "Twelve Year a Whore, five times a Wife... Twelve Year a Thief, Eight Year a Transported Felon..." Trutz is a *vivandière,* forager, combatant, wife to five officers, and the mistress of countless privates, and finally married to a gypsy. The relationship is obvious. Put Moll in a 17th century German army camp and she becomes Trutz with no effort at all.

There is a characteristic grossness and narrowing of perception among the German authors of *Schelmenroman,* as compared to Cervantes and Quevedo. The possible exception is *Ungarischer oder Dacianischer Simplicissimus* which appeared in 1683, to recreate Lazarillo as a wandering student who visits Constantinople, Egypt, Persia, and India, thereby combining education with amusement to the apparent satisfaction of the readers of that era.

The list of books is long, but the original contributions had already been made, and the remainder is chiefly repetition, piracy and adaptation. A considerable number of the later works were novels with a distinctly international flavor, and the pícaro wandered without apparent difficulty across oceans and deserts, always finding a handful of food and a new master. His sharp observation and cynical grasp of the realities of life seemed as applicable in Mongolia as in Madrid, and one has the feeling that he peeked under more tent flaps, and, especially in the *Schelmenroman,* more skirts than his Iberian counterpart.

As late as 1743 there was a flickering of the flame, when a *Simplicissimus Redivivus* was printed but, as in Spain, the genre had run its course in Germany. The writer would find nothing new to say through the pícaro's lips until the world had changed enough to provide him with new targets and new problems.

It should be understood that there was not one but rather a pair of distinct directions from which the pícaro reached Holland.

The political relations of the Lowlands with Spain made inevitable a cultural exchange, and *la novela picaresca* was far from the least of the items involved.

Translations were naturally the first introduction of the Iberian scamp to the stolid Dutch burghers, with *Celestina* in 1550 and *Lazarillo de Tormes* in 1579. The effect was long in becoming apparent, however, since the first reaction appears to have been Brederoo's comedy *Spaansche Brabander,* which was printed in 1617. Hooft followed suit in the same year with *Warenar,* which placed a picaro in Amsterdam, and in 1639 Huygen's *Klucht van Trijntje Cornelis* shifted the scene to Antwerp, and made the victim the wife of a Zaandam sailor.

Numerous translations followed, including French works as well as Spanish, since the social relations and geographical position of France made the works of Le Sage and others equally available. There appears to have been a definite Dutch trend toward embodying these characters and plots in drama, rather than in the novel, and it was not until 1695 that the first major novel of the class appears.

De Vermakelyke Avanturier, by Nicolass Heinsius, Jr. appeared in that year, and in it the doctor of medicine and philosophy combines picaro with adventurer. The protagonist begins in orthodox manner, in service with an inn-keeper, then a miserly lawyer, and the son of a Flemish nobleman, most of which is acceptably reminiscent of Lazarillo's boyhood. He then moves to high society in Paris, however, and ends as the steward of the French ambassador in London. The accent is upon romantic love, and the masters become a secondary interest, so that the satire is somewhat narrowed and more specifically slanted.

A highly significant difference is that the plot is well unified, and the loose, episodic nature of the Spanish original is lost. It was, however, reprinted eight times over a sixty-one year span, translated into French and Italian, and eventually raided by Jan van Hoogstraten for *De Geleerde Advokaat of de Bespotte Drüivedief* in 1707, and again for *De Verliefe Kok.*

The turn of the century found a renewed emphasis on translations of the Spanish classics, rather than original works, and the preference for adventure became increasingly apparent. Sentimentalism added further dilution, and the last purity was gone.

7

Pre-Lazarillo

Picaresque Elements

It has already been suggested that the rogue, who eventually became the Spanish pícaro, is a fundamental literary type, and the difference from era to era is largely topical, rather than psychological. Jonathan Wild was not troubled with Encolpius' homosexuality any more than Rinconete concerned himself with the political reforms which are so important to the *Chimaera seu Phantasma Mendicorum,* printed only six years later.

It is highly questionable whether there are many iden- tifiable lines of character and plot traceable directly from Greece and Rome to the *Siglo de Oro.* One may say without question that Shakespeare's Pistol is certainly descended from Plautus' Pyrgopolynices, the original Miles Gloriosus, but from what single character can one trace so complicated a personality as Guzmán de Alfarache? It is rather the rela- tionship of certain specific fictional characters (and, in some cases, perhaps not so fictional) to the societies in which they are portrayed, which continues into picaresque fiction.

To say "the original" with regard to any literary type is usually pointless, since one is immediately faced with the subjective question of real and false identification; perhaps the best approach is, therefore, to say "representative." And, of his period, surely one may say that of Aristophanes.

Without attempting a probably unnecessary explanation of

the status of a Greek personal slave, it should be noted that he was a "slave" often only in the legal sense, and came much closer to the modern concept of "paid companion." For example, the slave Xanthias in *The Frogs* has ample liberty to provide a rascally comic relief, which serves most effectively as a foil for Dionysus' clumsy maneuvering and cowardice. Although usually destitute, and to varying degrees limited in their capacity for independent action, Xanthias and many of his fellow slaves in Greece had already begun the long tradition of wits vs. wealth and, according to Aristophanes, they were on the winning side of this eternal struggle.

Continuing in the tradition of what eventually became picaresque comedy (to a Greek audience tragedy was not a fit subject for casual topical trifling) Plautus developed a basic plot which he used over and over again with only slight variations. One of the standard personalities in it was the lover's servant, a rascally, self-sufficient and quite unscrupulous type who helps the young master to gain the girl he loves, and in return receives his freedom.

This function, traditional and almost infinite in its possible variant forms, was customarily assigned to a male character in Plautine drama, since males in his society enjoyed a far greater freedom of movement, and therefore were capable of a greater contribution to the plot. In *Truculentus,* however, there is a reversal of the usual direction of events and the audience is presented with the picture of Phronesium, the courtesan, who calmly and deliberately plays each lover against all the others for added gains, much in the manner of a modern auctioneer.

The *Truculentus* is almost unique among Roman comedies so far as its bitter sardonic humor and realistic treatment of women in ancient society is concerned. Without discussing the specific characterization of Phronesium and her relationship to the *hataerae,* she is clearly a sister-at-heart of Celestina, and therein is to be found a direct connection between Rome and the *Siglo de Oro.*

Grismer has dealt with this problem at some length, eventually concluding that there was a strong influence on Fernando de Rojas by the Latin dramatists, Plautus in particular. The name Sosia in *La Celestina* is immediately suggestive of the scene in the *Amphitruo* in which Mercury impersonates him; the term *tragicomedia* used for *La Celestina* is highly unusual (Menéndez y Pelayo has pointed out that the word can be discovered only once between the two works) and the minor characteristic similarities are endless.

Plautus also made use of the parasite, and this individual, of which Peniculus is a fair example, may be considered a forerunner of the pícaro. This particular parasite is the comedian of the *Menaechmi,* which is a normal rôle for his character type. Even more amusing, however, is Ergasilus, whom Plautus perhaps developed to such an unusual degree in consideration of his particular function in the otherwise highly serious *Captivi.*

Between the slaves and the parasites of Plautus, it would be quite possible indeed to assemble a convincing pícaro and, to some extent, this is just what the Spanish and other European authors eventually did.

Returning to Plautus' specific topicalities, another and perhaps equally definite connection is Francisco Delicado's location of a street named *La via Asinaria* in *La Lozana Andaluzana.* This street is not on any modern street map of Rome and the suggestion of an indebtedness to the *Comedy of Asses* is irresistible.

Another possible Celestine indebtedness is to Seneca. The entire question of classical indebtedness is said to have begun with Barth's Latin translation in 1624,[1] and has continued into modern times with the labors of Menéndez y Pelayo, Cejador y Frauca, and Guisasola. The problem in this particular literary labor is, for once, not the dearth of material but rather the overwhelming supply.

That Seneca was well known in 16th century Spain, and even earlier, is shown by the translation of the *Senecae*

Proverbia into Spanish in 1482. Not less indicative is the fact that Seneca was referred to as *"el moral Séneca"* by Iberian disciples of the fifteenth century.

Other of his works were available, among which was the *Epistulae,* but the *Proverbia* was probably the most popular, and was certainly best represented in *La Celestina.* A detailed attempt at analyzing possible specific resemblances is beyond the scope of this discussion, but the general mood and philosophies of the Spanish closet drama and the bitter Roman's epigrams point up an unmistakable relationship.

Less specific in its resemblances to *picarismo,* but entirely in the same emotional pattern is *The Satyricon,* of Petronius Arbiter. Rome had changed greatly in its literary tastes by the first century A.D., and there was not only room but demand for the professional sensualist Petronius.

In the translation attributed to him Oscar Wilde categorizes *The Satyricon* with the statement: "Probably the nearest parallel of other literatures is the so called *Picaresque* romances of Spain, of which *Don Pablo of Segovia, Lazarillo de Tormes,* and if we regard it of Spanish origin, the incomparable *Gil Blas de Santillana* may be taken as typical examples."

It would seem highly significant that, in a twenty-seven page introduction, Wilde chose to mention only "Picaresque" romances as a social and emotional equivalent of *The Satyricon,* especially in view of the profound differences between Petronius and the picaresque writers in attitude toward sexual relationships, which were also a matter of such concern to Wilde. To him, apparently, the positive resemblances were so strong that they outweighed any differences.

Ernest A. Baker would appear to agree with this analysis since he comments emphatically, "Petronius was kept waiting for an English translator till late in the seventeenth century, when he was discovered to be a forerunner of the picaresque novelist."[2]

In contrast to Petronius, Apuleius learned Latin as an

adult, probably by much painful and deliberate effort, and he
therefore spoke the language much as European and Oriental
immigrants in modern times speak English, carefully, correctly, and in a manner normally unknown to the native of
their adopted country. Charles Whibley refers to Apuleius as
a "literary fop, conscious of his trappings and assured of a
handsome effect,"[3] but this may be somewhat unjust. The
author of *The Golden Ass* was indeed hyperconscious of
effect, but may this not be regarded simply as expert, diligent
writing? Perhaps it is as well that his literary efforts were
somewhat excessive, since William Adlington's translation in
1566 required a great deal of raw material if any genuinely
valuable result were to survive.

In any case, the plot remains intact, regardless of
Adlington's butchery, and it is the basic story which exhibits
a significant relationship to Lazarillo. The fact that the adventures, of a type which would be dubbed picaresque in
another fifteen hundred years, are experienced by the hero in
the form of a beast, does not alter the format. He is still a
frustrated, homeless wanderer at the mercy of an inimical
society, against which he has no weapon save his wits and his
bare body. Lazarillo would have called the ass "amigo"—and
then sold him to the nearest fence.

In both Petronius and Apuleius, one begins to sense the
growing Roman consciousness of an individual in conflict
with his society, and the possibility of living by one's wits if
there are no other resources available. Since this is the fundamental theme of all subsequent picaresque literature, it is
indeed tempting to chortle *"Quod erat demonstrandum"* and
retire from the field, but there is another aspect of predecessor literature which may be said to have a not
unimportant effect.

One standard didactic technique in Medieval Literature
was to personify a beast, and perhaps the most enduring of
these was Reynard, the Fox. Donald B. Sands refers to him as
a "folk hero"[4] and he might be so considered from a

noncritical point of view, but his amorality often falls far
short of the heroic, or even the acceptable.

The beast epic, which originated in the Low Countries in
the twelfth century, was a collection of animal tales, often in
verse and usually containing elements of both satire and didacticism.[5] The vulpine hero of *Reynard the Fox,* whose
name was taken, significantly, from the German
"Reindhardt" ("strong in counsel") is an outsider in an organized animal society to which he is attached (he never really
belongs). Sands defines him in part:

> He in no way represents the little man, even though he is a
> protagonist of average proportions. He would be inappropriate as
> a sociological or political symbol, despite the fact that his first
> and last impulse is to survive, and that he consistently portrays
> the innocently oppressed... He is human enough to possess a
> streak of genuine meanness, a degree of unpredictability, and a
> devastating flair for fake humility... It is possible to admire him,
> but in conventional circles we would perhaps hesitate to voice our
> admiration, for he is dangerously kin to our asocial selves.[6]

Unidentified, this might well serve as a thumbnail description
of Lazarillo, even though the "streak of genuine meanness"
must be assumed, since it is not portrayed. In other words,
the beast personifies the same social and personality orientation as the basic pícaro, and preceded him by some four
centuries.

The Middle English *Fox and the Wolf,* circa 1260, is really
a single episode from *Reynard.* While the incident per se of
outwitting a wolf, in order to use him as a well-bucket count-
erbalance, teaches no lesson applicable to *picarismo,* the
behavior of the fox is quite a different matter. By using his
wits he escapes from a dangerous situation at the expense of
a stronger but less intelligent competitor. The entire tale is
more than a little reminiscent of the *fabliau,* and still more of
the picaresque stories which will eventually succeed it.

It is quite possible, of course, to find isolated works which
can be used, by varying degrees of distortion, as apparent

predecessors, but the principal legitimate sources have already been mentioned.

The Seven Sages of Rome has been suggested in this context, along with any number of *fabliaux, exempla,* etc. The work most commonly cited as possibly suitable, and which this writer does not deem applicable, is the *Gesta Romanorum.* Regardless of the possible applicability of Moorish influence in introducing the book into the western European nations,[7] it is indisputable that this is the purest of didactic efforts, unconcerned with amusing the reader and intended for the preaching to and "profitable reading" by laymen. The picaresque novel's didacticism, on the other hand, was either accidental or hypocritical[8] and therein lies the irreconcilable difference. Unless the hypothetical source of the genre bears a distinct resemblance, either in detail or in spirit, there is little basis for identification, and the *Gesta Romanorum* shows neither.

One must remember that the writers of picaresque works were, almost without exception, men of some classical education or at least knowledge, and the Greek and Roman works mentioned as apparent sources were usually within their literary experience. This fact, continued into the following centuries, will render highly problematical the acknowledgement of indebtedness to any author who is himself indebted to a classic. If the chronological follower knew both an earlier writer's works, and the legends or tales upon which they were based, to which should the indebtedness be acknowledged?

8

The Pícaro in
British Literature

It seems clear that there was a perceptible effect of continental picaresque writings upon the English literature of those centuries following the printing of *Lazarillo de Tormes.* While this influence was not reflected in simple imitation and plot copying, which so commonly characterized the French and German tales, the spirit of the pícaro found easy passage from Madrid to London. Then too, while the desperately poor of England were common enough, they never displayed the hopeless fatalism of the Spaniard. It is this "never say die" attitude which is perhaps the greatest single difference between the two related literatures. Granting this "similarity with a difference," it would seem then that the problem is rather one of evaluation and identification of specific indebtedness.

It is difficult to establish a definite year for the first translation into English of *Lazarillo de Tormes,* even if one assumes the usual publication date of 1554.[1] Hardin Craig selects the earliest date of 1569,[2] de Morelos identifies the accomplishment as that of "David Roland" and dates it at 1576,[3] Chandler corrects the spelling to the more customary "Rowland" but endorses the date,[4] and Day chooses 1571 but gives no reason.[5] I suggest that perhaps the most useful evidence is that the book is shown on the *Stationers' Register* of 1568-1569 as "a boke intituled *the marvelus Dedes and the lyf of LAZARO DE TORMES.* "[6]

The work was, of course, available earlier in other languages, but in any case it was translated into English in ample time for the writers of the last decade of the 16th century. My intention at this point is simply to show that the story was readily available to Thomas Nashe before he published *The Unfortunate Traveller* in 1594 and this, in view of the above approximate consensus, seems evident. Whether Nashe "must have read it" as Craig rather rashly asserts is another matter. Baker modifies Craig by venturing that "Nashe may have heard of *Lazarillo de Tormes*...he may at least have known that it was written as an autobiography," and Hibbard completes the gamut somewhat belligerently with the flat challenge "there is nothing in Nashe's work to show that he had ever read *Lazarillo;* yet he never hesitated to borrow from such writings as he knew."

There is no evidence of which we are aware which will establish clearly whether Nashe did or did not have Lazarillo in mind when he fashioned Jack Wilton, and so the answer must come from the question, "Excluding the unlikely possibility of totally original conception, from what more likely source might Nashe have taken his hero"?

It is surely inconceivable that a prominent literary figure so involved in the literature of his day as Thomas Nashe had never read the new and revolutionary *Lazarillo de Tormes,* especially since it had been available in English for more than twenty years. Hibbard's contention seems illogical, since it is based entirely upon the absence of direct borrowing in *The Unfortunate Traveller*. By this he apparently means specific incidents, names, places, etc., since he could not possibly mean to imply that there is no similarity in philosophy between the two youths. Lazarillo's skepticism of his elders and betters, his gutter-brat realism in dealing with noble ideas, and his total lack of sympathy for pain and sorrow are repeated by Jack again and again, in a score of incidents. While *The Unfortunate Traveller* may, as Hibbard asserts, start out as a jest-book, it quickly turns into what must be considered a novel, historical and picaresque, and it is in this form that it continues and concludes. And it is this aspect which, in the opinion of this writer, constitutes a distinct and direct indebtedness to *Lazarillo de Tormes.*

It is possible that this argument may be essentially semantic in nature, and soluble by differentiating between *copying* and *indebtedness.* That Nashe scorned the former is clear—his mind and imagination were entirely adequate to his needs, and he found Italy a much more fertile field for English contempt than Spain (although Iberian clothing, food and bedding all come in for a fair share of thrusts).[7] Nashe had no need to copy, however, and so he didn't!

Is the extent of possible indebtedness, however, to copy in a direct and traceable manner? If so, what term should then be used for inspiration or mood derived from the *spirit* of a literary work? The former is surely an excessively limited definition, and indebtedness may be considered to include the idea and spirit of the work, in addition to or instead of specific minutiae. It is the spirit of Lazarillo which is to be found in *The Unfortunate Traveller.* As Baker puts it, "a peculiar attitude to life happened to coincide with a streak of humor in the English temperament, and a very effective way of expressing it found a ready response in English writers."[8]

Chandler devotes a full seven pages to this apparent indebtedness, but he contributes no more than a summary of the several arguments. His most significant statement appears to be, "It is the earliest English fiction of pretension in the picaresque genre."[9]

Jusserand refers to *The Unfortunate Traveller,* in connection with *Lazarillo de Tormes,* by commenting that "original romances of this kind were published here, among others, by Thomas Nashe, in the sixteenth [century]"[10] and eventually concludes that "Jack Wilton [is] the best specimen of the picaresque tale in English literature anterior to Defoe."[11]

The question seems, then, to be the *type* of indebtedness, rather than its existence, and it must be concluded that, while Nashe was apparently inspired and intrigued by the concept of the pícaro, who takes form in English as Jack Wilton, Jack is by no means a remodeled Lazarillo. He was, however, the first of the rogue-heroes of the English novel, and whether or not one agrees with Chandler that Jack Wilton was also the last one of literary merit for more than a century, there is no question that his example was both permanent and exciting.

There is one major difference, however, which must be emphasized since it indicates the new direction which is to be followed by English writers for many generations to come. It has been pointed out that the Spanish picaresque novel was not intentionally didactic, and that the author's intent was simply to tell a good tale. This is definitely not true of *The Unfortunate Traveller.* It will be one hundred and fifty-five years before Henry Fielding declares "I shall not look on myself as accountable to any court of critical jurisdiction whatever; for as I am, in reality, the founder of a new province of writing, so I am at liberty to make what laws I please therein."[1 2] Nashe felt this so deeply that he did not even bother to mention it.

In consequence, his hatred of the Anabaptists, his typical disapproval of the Italianate Englishman, his excessive larding of the story with Latin tags are all given such space as he chooses that they shall have, and he has no hesitation in using the story as a vehicle for any preaching he wishes to do. This practice will prove to be the rule, rather than the exception, in English writing of the next era and it is perhaps the most basic redirection of the picaresque.

For approximately the next seventy years there appears to have been an hiatus in the production of original picaresque literature, during which much translation appeared, and a quantity of romantic sentimentalism. Such efforts as portraying the pícaro as Humphrey Crouche's,[1 3] showed him rather as victim and fool and, while many of the exploits of the hero Taffie reflect Spanish and German originals, the spirit of the pícaro is entirely absent.

It was not until 1663 that it reappeared, when first Richard Head, then Francis Kirkman, and finally both contributed to that wretched effort which is *The English Rogue.* It is quite impossible to discuss these two writers in the sense of evaluating their literary skill, since neither possessed any. They were money-hungry hacks, whose sole idea was to produce an ultra-rogue story, without any regard for authenticity, morality, or literary value.

To be sure, the work was not without its supporters. In fact, a misguided admirer, identified only as "N.D.," provided the following dubious compliment, which Head immediately affixed to Part One of the story:

> Guzman, Lazaro, Buscon, and Francion,
> Til thou appear'dst did shine as at high Noon.
> Thy Book's now extant; those that judge of Wit,
> Say, They and Rabelais too fall short of it.[14]

The hero of the story is one Meriton Latroon. Although I am not aware of other opinions on the subject, it seems possible that the name is an Anglicization of the Spanish *ladrón*, which is thief. A nation which could produce "Bazelus manus"[15] would surely not have quailed at this!

The tale itself includes many incidents of gratuitous crime and villainy, which completely nullify Francis Kirkman's attempt at justification:

> if the readers had the Spanish Rogue Gusman; the French Rogue Francion; and several others by foreign wits and have upon examination found that the authors were persons of great eminency and honour, and that no part of their own writings were their own lives, they had happily changed their opinions of the author of this...[16]

and again when he tries to deny the viciousness of his hero:

> Rogue did I call him? I should recall that word, since his actions were attended more with witty concepts, than life-destroying stratagems. It is to conceit, the whole bend of his

mind tended to little else than Exhorbitancy; and necessity
frequently compelled him to perpetrate villainy...[17]

There is some justification for this statement, but not a
great deal. The truth is that Meriton Latroon uses half the
tricks in the picaresque literature of Spain, Italy, Germany,
Holland, France and finally England. He draws upon the jest-
books, Awdeley's *Fraternatie of Vacabondes,* Harmon's
Caveat for Common Cursitors and anything else at hand, and
the purpose is often outright evil, without any possible
"necessity."

Wilbur L. Cross makes the point that *The English Rogue*
continues the practice of sending English picaros to foreign
countries,[18] which becomes almost a standard practice.
Defoe, Fielding, and Smollett will use this device as the basic
part of the plot of many works, and eventually the genre will
come to include entire stories presenting the autobiography
of a citizen of a foreign country, such as Hajji Babba,
Anastasius and Pandurang Hàrì.

Possibly the most interesting part of *The English Rogue* is
the seven page "canting vocabulary."[19] It contains 87 words
and phrases and may be related to the *Rothwelsch* vocabulary included in the *Liber Vagatorum.* It should, however, be
noted that Harmon included the same sort of information in
the *Caveat for Common Cursitors,* and this appears a more
likely and immediately available source for the unscholarly
Head and Kirkman.

In any case, the purpose of this investigation is picaresque
identification, not literary criticism, and that *The English
Rogue* is clearly in the pattern is not to be questioned.
Although Latroon often exceeds the normal activities of the
Spanish picaro, and the romantic erotic portion of his activities is somewhat emphasized, the former is the exception
rather than the rule, and the erotic element will prove to be
characteristic of the entire procession of the 18th century
English novel.

The two works just discussed comprise almost the entire
output of Renaissance and Restoration picaresque novels

produced in England, and it is not until well in the 18th century that another major original effort appears. There was, of course, a continuing stream of more or less accurate translation of original Spanish works, but by this time such material was sufficiently common that there was no problem of its availability to Daniel Defoe when he produced *Moll Flanders* in 1722. The question, in his case, is the extent to which it was influential.

In the case of Thomas Nashe, the influence must have come from *Lazarillo de Tormes* or nowhere, since this was the only work which was surely available to Nashe before 1594. Defoe, on the other hand, had almost the entire Spanish picaresque canon available in English translation, and there is no reason why Moll should show any particular resemblance to Lazarillo. Her prototype, if there was one, may have been *La Pícara Justina* by Andrés Pérez. There appears to be some disagreement about the translation, Chandler giving the title as *The Spanish Libertines*[20] and Cross *The Country Jilt*,[21] although both identify the translator as Stevens, and the date as 1707. Some verismilitude is lent to Cross' version by the mention in George Coleman's farce *Polly Honeycomb* (1760) of one hundred and eighty-two contemporary works, including *The Jilts, or the Female Fortune Hunters*.[22] At any rate, this specific work was available to Defoe in translation. *Celestina* was too, so far as that goes, but since there is no apparent relationship between Moll and the old procuress, it need not be considered further. The only other work which might bear on the question is *Trutz Simplex,* but while there is a definite resemblance between Justina and Trutz, there is less between Trutz and Moll. It may be concluded, therefore, that if there is picaresque indebtedness, it is to *La Pícara Justina.*

Martin S. Day refers to Moll as "the most famous female picaroon in English literature."[23] This statement is unclear, since if he is intentionally differentiating between "female picaroon" and "pícara" then his intention must be to emphasize the criminal instead of the picaresque. "Picaroon" does not exist in the common Spanish idiom,[24] and so far as this writer has been able to determine, in English it implies a female pirate rather than rogue.[25] If this is Day's meaning, it is open to debate, since the actual female pirates, such as Anne Bonney, had a far greater reputation in the 18th century, if not in our own. If he meant to imply "pícara" we are back at the *Siglo de Oro,* and in agreement.

This is not to suggest that there is no other logical background which might explain Defoe's direction; for one thing it might have been based upon first-hand experience acquired in Newgate, where he was imprisoned in 1703 for writing "The Shortest Way with Dissenters." The authenticity of *Moll Flanders* might strongly endorse this theory, were it not that Defoe had the gift of writing with such convincing realism about events which had never happened, at least to him.

A more likely source of information was Defoe's employment by John Applebee as a writer for "Applebee's Journal" in which criminals' confessions and biographies were featured. This was during the period of Defoe's "picaresque" writings, and his frequent association with rogues might have had a distinct effect on the style and content of his works.

Regardless of these possibilities, it remains fundamentally true that *Moll Flanders* is in the direct tradition of the pícara, and reflects its limitations and rules. Raleigh goes a step further in stating that Defoe's later works also include samples of the picaresque romance, such as *Colonel Jack* (1722) and *Roxana* (1724),[26] but these books are less evident of indebtedness than is *Moll Flanders.* Furthermore, they are simple variants on the basic theme and it is in the additions to the original picaresque type that Defoe's work is most significant.

There are two basic variations which deserve consideration:

First, Moll Flanders is utterly devoid of humor. This was a change in the picaresque, however, not in Defoe, since there was no humor in any of his works. Nevertheless, the authors of the picaresque novels of the past had always looked upon life as a rather grim jest, some with the accent on the adjective and some with it on the noun, but always admitting the justice of both. Defoe, on the other hand, denied the humor of life, and this left only the grimness without the relief of even a wry smile.

Secondly, Moll's designer makes her a human being, which never before had happened in a picaresque tale. For the first time a pícara makes the fatal mistake of falling in love, and almost the entire problem of Moll is traceable to her human feelings in one form or another. Chandler comments that "Moll Flanders experiences all the hopes and fears of a blind devotion."[27] This is not to be taken to mean that Moll is either soft or fine; far from it, she is basically a whore, and her happy end is as little her fault as is her miserable career.[28] The difference is that she was never able to cultivate the fine suppression of conscience which had previously been so characteristic of the pícara.

Moll Flanders is didactic in intent, but it has already been pointed out that this may be regarded as a characteristic of the English picaresque type. It is, of course, entirely normal in Defoe (*Robinson, Crusoe* is really a king-sized sermon) and Moll would have been intended to preach even if Nashe's Jack Wilton had not. Almost every 18th and 19th century English novel had the sermon lurking somewhere in it, and, in fact, most Victorians considered this the only justification for the genre.

There was no need for the sermon to hide its head when Samuel Richardson produced *Pamela*, however, since to any reader who can overlook the pruriency of the heroine's preoccupation with marriage, the entire book is a moral lecture.

Chandler relates the story to the picaresque on the basis of a heroine in service, and the author's attention to commonplace detail, but this writer cannot endorse the classification. By 1740 the serving maid was sufficiently common in fiction that her presence proved nothing. Unlike the pícara, who is always alone in her world, Pamela never is. In evaluating any picaresque aspects or indebtedness in the story, it seems more important that Pamela has two living parents, of whom the reader is repeatedly made aware, with whom she is in close contact and, save for a period of literal imprisonment, to whom she can return whenever she chooses; she is employed, and with the exception of Mrs. Jewkes and Squire−, does not live in a hostile world.

Attention to commonplace detail is surely not a uniquely picaresque element, since by mid-18th century there is a strong trend toward realism in the novel, which is so wide-spread that the general indebtedness is no longer significant when it appears in any certain work.

A further denial of picaresqueness is the epistolary format which, in a story told in the present tense, as is true of Pamela, precludes a resemblance. Pícaras are too busy to write letters, even if they should know how to write, and have no one to read them in any case. It is more reasonable, therefore, to regard Richardson as a separate minute genre, and to search elsewhere for Lazarillo.

The search is short, since Henry Fielding began producing genuine picaresque works three years later. (It is true that *Shamela*[29] does not fit this frame, but it was intended as a burlesque of *Pamela,* and is subject to the same stylistic limitations.)

Doubtless drawing upon his police-court experiences as a magistrate, Fielding produced *Joseph Andrews* within another year and there should be no reasonable doubt of the direct picaresque relationship even if the author had not carefully expressed his indebtedness to Cervantes on the title page of his novel.[30] Although Joseph is in no sense a Sancho Panza, the quixotic nature of Parson Adams is unquestionable. If the purpose of this study were the identification of resemblance, rather than indebtedness, there might be some room for doubt, since Joseph is far too innocent and naïve to share a crust with Lazarillo. It is indebtedness with which the discussion is concerned, however, and there can be no doubt that both the trip and the personality of Parson Adams are directly traceable to the *Siglo de Oro.*

If stealing, lying, cheating and general immorality are the requirement, then the place to seek for them is in Fielding's very next work. Jonathan Wild organizes a school for apprentice criminals, informs on them for blood money, and stops at nothing for personal gain. Fielding himself describes his protagonist as "A scoundrel"[31] and there are few who would debate his right to the title.

It is quite true that his self-education by means of picaresque tales is an indication, and Fielding tells his readers that "the Spanish Rogue was his favorite book, and the Cheats of Scapin his favorite play." Furthermore, the author codifies his hero's basis of relationships with others, including the following:

1. Never to do more mischief to another than was necessary to the effecting of his purpose.

(This study has already suggested that the pícaro is characterized by "restraining from deliberate violence for its own sake..."[32])

2. To know no distinction of men from affection, but to sacrifice all with equal readiness to his interest.

(It is surely obvious that the basic interest of a pícaro is to obtain employment with a good master, and affection is a luxury which a Lazarillo cannot afford. The pícaro therefore takes service with anyone who will have him, and asks no more than that the master can support him.)

3. To forgive no enemy, but to be cautious and often dilatory in revenge.

(Lazarillo says, "So I decided to finish him off instead. But I didn't set about it right away. I waited till I could do it safely and make a good job of it."[33])

The remaining 12 points in Jonathan Wild's code of conduct for "attaining greatness" are equally applicable to the essential pícaro, since they deal with such matters as never trusting one who has deceived you, nor one whom you have already deceived, keeping affection on your face and hatred in your heart, and that virtues, like precious stones, are easily counterfeited and equally decorative in both cases. Lazarillo or Celestina would, one suspects, concur heartily in every item!

There seems, then, to be a basis of identification of Jonathan Wild with the picaresque, yet there is another aspect which must be considered. It has been noted that the pícaro usually wins his battle with life, and is alive to tell his story at the end, often as a reformed, virtuous citizen. In contrast, Jonathan Wild is hanged as a criminal!

The question, therefore, is whether the clear general resemblance to the picaresque is invalidated by the violation of a tenet of the definition.

This is a significant point, since the decision will constitute a precedent in dealing with Smollett, Thackeray, Kipling, and eventually Steinbeck, Hemingway, Faulkner and numerous others. It is the question of flexibility in applying the criterion, and must be answered now.

In the opinion of this writer, there is almost no single standard or model which is fully applicable to all possible variants of any subject, and the result to be expected from excessive rigidity is an invariable negative. On the other hand, the word "indebtedness" suggests that any significant, applicable resemblance to an earlier work should be considered a positive correlation, and acknowledged accordingly. This is not meant to imply that it should not be a carefully qualified acknowledgement, such as that of *Jonathan Wild* is intended to be.

Taking this as an example, therefore, the opinion of this writer is that there are unmistakable indications in the book that the author was well aware of picaresque characteristics, and was consciously influenced by them when he created the personality of his hero. Aurelien Digeon, in his comprehensive analysis of Fielding as a novelist, confirms this attitude when he concludes "*Jonathan Wild* is essentially a picaresque novel, the offspring of an ancient tradition."[34] Furthermore, Fielding has elsewhere deliberately acknowledged such indebtedness to Cervantes, which can only mean that he wishes the erudite reader to be aware of this relationship and to look for it.

On this basis, it would appear that Jonathan Wild may indeed be considered a pícaro, and later works will be considered and evaluated in accordance with the same criterion.

Fielding reached the peak of his fiction-writing career when he produced *Tom Jones,* and this is emphasized by the manner in which he used the picaresque elements which he had practiced in *Joseph Andrews* and *Jonathan Wild,* Chandler comments perceptively that "*Tom Jones,* indeed, though it could scarcely have come into being without picaresque predecessors, transcends them all,"[35] and with this statement there can be little disagreement. When, however, he continues by saying that the novel cannot be ranked with the literature of roguery, there is room for considerable doubt. It is true that the entire story is not picaresque, but then few English novels were.

One of the more significant innovations of this work is that it is divided into three or perhaps even four distinct periods in the hero's life, and while they form a unity before the story ends, they are not all written in the same vein. Of particular interest to the present discussion are books VII through XII, the period of Tom's trip to London from the Somersetshire estate of Squire Allworthy. In this journey the hero becomes increasingly the vehicle of social satire and it is then that he is of the Lazarillos of this world. It is true that even, in these circumstances, Tom remains an individual rather than a "type," such as Cervantes and Le Sage aimed at, but stylization is not necessarily characteristic of the

pícaro—how could one be more individual than Guzmán or
Celestina?

There is no question that Fielding's art as a writer greatly
exceeded the admittedly restricting bounds of the picaresque
novel but, in the opinion of this writer, his works show a
distinct picaresque influence which seasoned his literary pie,
and without which much of his work would have been less
than it is.

One of the several important points which Fielding and
Tobias Smollett appear to share is a hero with distinctly
picaresque characteristics, based upon an identifiable Spanish
model, even though Fielding did not exhibit the limited
ability and lack of understanding which so characterizes
Smollett's novels. As Cross comments with more point than
gentleness:

> Fielding and Smollett have much in common; a novel as they
> conceived of it, is a union of intrigue and adventure. But in the
> disposition of their material they were far apart. Fielding when at
> his best grouped and arranged incidents for dramatic effect, with
> his final chapter in view. Smollett, too, brought his stories to a
> close in the manner of *Tom Jones*, with a marriage and a descrip-
> tion of the charms of the bride: yet there was no logic in this; it
> was merely a mechanical device for stopping somewhere. Smol-
> lett's novels are strings of adventure and personal histories, and it
> is not quite clear to the reader why they might not be shuffled
> into any other succession than the one they have assumed.[36]

This is fair criticism indeed, but it suggests something quite
different as well.

A loosely constructed, episodic tale is one of the most
characteristic common denominators of the picaresque genre,
and it is surely not unreasonable to suggest that an author
who in a single chapter of a novel mentions *Guzmán de
Alfarache, Don Quixote,* Scarron and *Gil Blas* is subject to
their stylistic influence.[37]

This interpretation is, in part, supported by G.H.
Maynadier in his introductory evaluation of Smollett. He
comments:

It does not follow that *Roderick Random* as a work of art is almost without faults; far from it: but the faults are mostly those of the literary type to which it belongs,–the so-called picaresque novel. This peculiar kind of fiction, which came into existence in Spain in the sixteenth century, differed from the old romances of chivalry not so much in form as in substance. In both, the author apparently got tired of further additions, and summarily brought the hero to his desired end.[38]

Smollett's literary model was Le Sage, whose *Gil Blas* he translated in 1749. *Roderick Random,* in particular, seems a definite effort to copy, if not to some degree, paraphrase *Gil Blas.* Smollett himself acknowledges this in his preface to *Roderick Random,* when he admits:

> The same method has been practiced by other Spanish and French authors, and by none more successfully than by Monseiur Le Sage, who, in his *Adventures of Gil Blas* has described the knavery and foibles of life, with infinite humor and sagacity. The following sheets I have modeled on his plan.[39]

Roderick is, indeed, a seagoing Gil Blas to a perceptible degree, and there are much the same, if fewer, traces in *Peregrine Pickle* Neither is a great novel, even if Smollett was wise enough to use incidents from Fielding's works, as well as those of Le Sage and Scarron. Even in *The Adventures of Ferdinand, Count Fathom* (1753), there is a consciousness of Fielding as well as the Spanish and French writers, for Smollett, while carefully avoiding the mention of Jonathan Wild's creator, nevertheless complains about readers:

> who extol the writings of Petronius Arbiter, read with rapture the amorous sallies of Ovid's pen, and chuckle over the story of Lucian's ass: yet, if a modern author presumes to relate the progress of a simple intrigue, are shocked at the indecency and immorality of the scene;–who delight in following Guzman d'Alfarache through all the mazes of squalid beggary; who with pleasure accompany Don Quixote and his squire in the lowest paths of fortune; who are diverted with the adventures of Scarron's ragged troop of strollers; and highly entertained with the servile situations of Gil Blas; yet when a character in humble

life occasionally occurs in a performance of our own growth
exclaims with an air of disgust,—'Was ever anything so mean!
Surely this writer must have been very conservant with the lowest
scenes of life!'[40]

While thus warning his readers, Smollett manages to point
up the influence of the picaresque on his own art, and to
hold himself absolved from personal taint. Considering what
was to follow in the novel, this was perhaps a wise pre-
caution.

The book itself is often revealing of the extent to which
Smollett was indebted to his predecessors, since their names
come easily to his pen whenever occasion offers; for example,
he refers to one of Count Fathom's messmates as "an odd
sort of man, a kind of Lazarillo de Tormes."

Baker refers to the book as "a sort of picaresque novel
having a thorough-going miscreant instead of a genial rogue as
its central figure"[41] and this is a good definition. The novel
has, however, an excessive didactic emphasis, and it has
already been noted that preaching is not the primary purpose
of the picaresque. Baker emphasizes this when he comments
that "Smollett committed the capital mistake of twisting to
didactic purposes a story that should have been told either in
the spirit of devil-may-care picaresque comedy, or the cool
irony of Fielding's Jonathan Wild."[42]

Oddly enough, Chandler sets aside the hero in favor of the
horrid mother, whom he chooses to include by stating that it
is in her that "the Spanish picaresque spirit really prevailed."
There is, of course, a ring of Justina in her behavior, for she is
indeed a camp follower, whore and thief, but a debatable
point arises when the reader is told that she is in the habit of
going about the battlefield with a poniard, dispatching
wounded soldiers in order to steal their personal possessions.
She is, in fact, eventually killed by a wounded hussar who
declines to let her murder him for the sake of the costly
standard which he has captured.

The tradition of the pícara has never included habitual

murder, and Celestina, Trutz, Justina and their sisters do not include it in their repertoires. For this reason, the actions of Fathom *mère* raise a real question. Chandler himself appears to forget that it was he who codified the distinction:

> As the typical crime of the villain is murder, so the typical crime of the rogue is theft... But the use of personal violence usually ends his career as rogue, and stamps him the villain.[43]

It would appear therefore that, while Count Fathom's mother may exhibit certain picaresque traits, she is no pícara.

In 1755 Smollett reasserted his intimate relationship with the *Siglo de Oro* by translating his beloved "Don Quixotte" into English. Whether it was, as has been suggested, only a rehash of Jarvis' 1742 translation, even an improved one, there seems little doubt that it was at least indirectly responsible for *The Adventures of Sir Launcelot Greaves,* which appeared in serialized form in 1760. One reason for the editorial acceptance of this admittedly mediocre work may have been that Smollett and Goldsmith were the managers of the magazine. The story itself has little to recommend it. It was, however, the first of a long line of English serialized novels, and the style was obviously designed to permit this mode of publication.

The original *Don Quijote* is not a picaresque work, even taking into account Sancho Panza's problems, and Timothy Crabshaw does not make one of Launcelot Greaves. The indebtedness is clear, in this case, but it is to a single work—not to the picaresque tradition.

When, however, Smollett wrote *The History and Adventures of an Atom* in 1769, he was working in a tradition which was really a picaresque sub-genre: the tale of the Inanimate Hero. Although Fielding, after whom Smollett trudged in unending imitation, had published the *Journey from this World to the Next* in 1743, this was not necessarily the prototype for Smollett's novel, since both men were *aficionados* of the Spanish picaresque and must have known

Antonio Enriquez Gómez' *Siglo Pitagórico,* which could have served them both.

Steele used this principle of picaresque reincarnation, substituting transmigration of soul for transfer between masters, in the *Tatler*[44] and Addison did the same in the *Spectator.*[45] It is in the latter, especially, that the idea is most fully developed, since a monkey allegedly describes his adventures as both beast and man, having carefully explained that he was granted the gift of remembering his previous incarnations. The picaresque is particularly apparent since the author of the latter work, who uses the monkey for his own purposes, is trying to impress a young lady—a trick worthy of Jack Wilton or Jonathan Wild!

Fielding used the traditional device of the "manuscript found in an attic" and let it describe the adventures of Julian the Apostate as he transmigrates through some twenty-one incarnations. Smollett, for once, improved on Fielding; his "hero" did not require a human body, and therein lay one of his advantages—unlimited versatility. The protagonist is, accordingly, in turn a part of such diverse forms as a salad, a Dutch sailor, a duck, an Englishman and the editor's own father. Equating "master" and "incarnation" produces a definite variety of picaresque, and this is, perhaps, the most imaginative if not the most artistic of Smollett's writings.

Raleigh has defined this particular application of the picaresque by noting:

> a certain limitation is imposed on the...picaresque form by the necessity of bringing all the events recorded within the cognizance of the hero... But to bring all these scenes under the observation of one hero...sometimes proved difficult or impossible. In good time, therefore, a new and looser form was invented... A guinea or a hymn-book can with perfect propriety be present at scenes into which it would be difficult to introduce a dispassionate human observer. Let the guinea or hymn-book be endowed with the power of speech, and the last restraint is taken off social and personal satire.[46]

One of the earliest of these works was *The History of Pompey the Little, or the Life and Adventures of a Lap-Dog,* written by Francis Coventry in 1751, in which satirical portraits of well-known persons are connected by a rather thin plot. Charles Johnstone, upon the recommendation of Doctor Johnson, produced a satire of the Seven Years War in *Chrysal, or the Adventures of a Guinea* (1769). His plot traces the gold of a coin from a mine in Peru, to a Jesuit who receives it from a Peruvian sailor, and follows the already soiled bit of metal through its arrival in London. The movement of the coin from one master to another is exactly analogous to that of a picaresque servant, and the comments on owners are almost interchangeable with those which Lazarillo might have made about his priests and *hidalgos.*

The Adventures of a Black Coat was published in the same year, and was followed by a host of others, including the *Adventures of a Bank-note* (1770), the *Life and Adventures of a Cat* (1781), the *Adventures of a Ruppee* (1782) and the *Memoirs of a Flea* (1785). The list of objects used for this purpose is almost endless, and one finds "Adventures of..." such things as a Fly, Horse, Little White Mouse, Pincushion, Corkscrew, Peg Top, Whipping Top, Silver Threepence, Air Balloon, Hackney Coach, Pin and finally an "Ostrich Feather of Quality."

None of this type has lasted as literature, and those which we still know, such as Fielding's and Smollett's, continue to be found on library shelves out of regard for the authors' other works, not for the intrinsic worth of the specific books. Nevertheless, they reflected a particular picaresque element, and helped to pass it on to the writers of better books which were to come.

Not to be considered among these, but nevertheless in the same chronological period, was John Cleland's *Memoirs of a Woman of Pleasure* which appeared in 1769. Cleland himself is reputed, at least according to James Boswell, to have been the model for Will Honeycomb of *Spectator* fame,[47] but this is not substantiated. There can be no question, however, that Cleland was one of the "anti-Pamela" authors, whose annoyance with Richardson found expression in other works such as Fielding's[48] and John Kelly's spurious sequel.[49]

Whether Fanny Hill is intended to amplify Moll Hackabout,[50] or whether they are simply the result of the same social conditions, is open to debate. It cannot be doubted, however, that Fanny is in the most direct line of descent from Justina. It has been pointed out, and bears repetition at this point, that the pícara may enjoy sex, but she is not a whore from choice, and sheds the rôle as soon as the opportunity is offered. Fanny is tricked into the profession, and remains in it only as long as she must. As soon as she has sufficient funds she sets up as a gentlewoman and leads a life which she has limited to "such lines of life and conduct as, leaving me a competent library to pursue my views, either out of pleasure or fortune, bounded me nevertheless strictly within the rules of decency and discretion."[51] Thus the image of the pícara is maintained, and it is Fanny's eventual reunion with her original lover which makes the story's point: true love is an excuse for lust. The moral issue enters into neither the book nor this study—one may, if he chooses, accept Cleland's premise, and no doubt he will then find no objection to the conclusions.

Cleland's other books, such as *Memoirs of a Coxcomb, Surprises of Love, The Man of Honor,* etc., are of little greater literary value, and have scarcely more appeal than his *Specimen of an Etymological Vocabulary or Essay by means of the Analytic Method, to retrieve the Ancient Celtic.*

After Cleland's notorious story there followed a seventy year period of adventure stories, almost all having some identifiable picaresque elements, but none of which has survived on its literary merits. The story of the destitute youth who enlists in the army or navy, goes to London to seek his fortune, joins a gypsy band or participates in one of the other traditional gambits to appear eventually as a hero, became eventually routine, rather than unique, and it was only the details of the format which differed.

Most Englishmen of the period apparently equated Spanish with picaresque, and accordingly lumped Don Quijote into a sort of Iberian potpourri along with Lazarillo, Guzmán, and Justina. For example, Mrs. Lennox published a *Female Quixote* in 1752, which is described as a romance:

> in which the heroine Arabella, the only child of a widowed and misanthropic marquis, is supposed to be brought up in seclusion in the country, where she has access to a library full of old romances, by which her head is almost as much turned as that of the Knight of La Mancha was by the same kind of study. She takes a young gardener in her father's service for a nobleman in disguise, and is with difficulty undeceived when he gets a thrashing for stealing carp from a pond.[52]

Included in that group of authors to which Mrs. Lennox belongs are Johnstone, Henry Brooks, William Godwin, and Mrs. Inchbald, none of whom is of significance in picaresque or, for that matter, any type of English literature.

It was not until 1819 that the pícaro again took the center of the stage, this time in Thomas Hope's *Anastasius, or Memoires of a Greek at the Close of the Eighteenth Century.* The influence in this case is clearly Le Sage, and everything but the undesirable sentimentality can be traced to Gil Blas. Anastasius is in service as a soldier of fortune during most of the story, rather than as a servant, but this change of occupation does not interfere with the clear picaresque overtone.

Day refers to the book as a "belated specimen of the picaresque tale,"[53] but this appears to ignore its significant position in both the genre and its influence on the English novel.

The importance of *Anastasius* is that it is the first of a series of books by Englishmen, dealing with oriental picaresque heroes, and professing to understand the Eastern psychology and mode of life. It is highly doubtful that all of them do, although some of the material is clearly based upon either good personal observation or reliable accounts. In few cases, however, did the author have the intimate knowledge of the society about which he wrote, which is so characteristic of the work of Fielding and Defoe. The result is a type of factually-based fairy tale, into which the picaro fits easily and naturally, just as he might into "Jack and the Beanstalk" or "Robin Hood."

A work in this vein, and of considerably greater literary merit than *Anastasius,* is *The Adventures of Hajji Baba of Ispahan,* which was finished by James Morier in 1824. It is one of the few oriental picaresque tales based upon personal experience, since Morier was the son of a British Consul in Constantinople, and himself later spent a total of seven years in Persia. His knowledge of the life of his characters was therefore genuine, even if one may suspect that their motives were often as incomprehensible to Morier as to his English audience.

The author was determined to create a picaresque story from the very beginning, since the introductory letter from a fictitious storyteller explains:

> I then suggested, that perhaps if a European would give a correct idea of Oriental Manners...perhaps the best method would be to...work them into one connected narrative, upon the plan of that excellent picture of European Life, 'Gil Blas' of Le Sage.

Hajji Baba begins his career by leaving his father's barber shop to take service with a Turkish trader, and becomes the complete Lazarillo as he passes through a full cycle of situations as servant, soldier, captive, etc. and in the process finds occasion to comment upon the habits and shortcomings not only of his own social and professional groups, but of all others with which he comes in contact.

This work was so well received that Morier made the common mistake of attempting the sequel at which he had hinted at the end of his first book, and in 1828 he produced

The Adventures of Hajji Baba of Ispahan in England. This tale is in no sense picaresque, since Hajji is now a member of the Persian Ambassador's suite, and the format is much closer to Goldsmith's *Citizen of the World* than to *Gil Blas.* Morier's subsequent works are sentimental, rather than picaresque, and it must therefore be concluded that only in his original book is the influence evident.

Another effort of this type, *Pandurang Hàri, or the Memoirs of a Hindoo,* appeared in 1826, the third of its oriental format within seven years. The author is usually considered to be William Browne Hockley, but this is not emphasized since the story is presented as the translation of a manuscript. Whether it really is or whether the explanation is the same device used by Hawthorne in *The Custom-House* cannot be determined.

Pandurang Hàri begins in a clearly picaresque vein, when the young boy is thrown at the age of five into a hostile world to find his own way. This is emphasized by:

> a servant, who pestered me with questions which I could not answer; demanding who I was? whence I came? who were my parents? to which, of course, I was unable to make any reply than *malla towak n,hae* ("I know not").[54]

The boy passes through a series of services, beginning with Sawunt Rao Copal Rao, commander of a division of the army, and continuing with much of Indian society and government. His story is finally told as a dying man, safe in England, and this is again a standard pattern in the picaresque novel.

That this type of story was recognized as picaresque by the critics and readers of the day is pointed up by a list of "Works Published by Henry S. King & Co." included in the edition cited above, which mentions the following undated quotation from the London *Times:*

> There is a quaintness and simplicity in the roguery that makes his life as attractive as that of Guzman d'Alfarache or Gil Blas.

These three oriental pícaros were followed by a group of English lads, continuing in the same vein of "rags to riches" adventure tale. It has been suggested by Chandler and others that, for example, Bulwer's *Paul Clifford* is an "adapted" picaresque novel—a term totally unpalatable to this writer. *Picarismo* may certainly be present in greater or lesser degrees, but it does not permit "adaptation" any more than does any other generic literary form.

Paul Clifford, far from being a pícaro, is an unjustly condemned man who turns to crime and revenge. The emphasis in the book is a sort of Gothic satire, and the intent is clearly didactic, rather than amusing. Bulwer himself said so when he declared that the purpose of the work was "to draw attention to two errors in our penal institutions, viz: a vicious Prison Discipline and a sanguinary Penal Code."[54] This is a social reform he preaches, and there is no place for Lazarillo in that crusading society, which will presently be labeled Victorian.

Ainsworth was, in *Rookwood,* no more in the picaresque tradition than was Bulwer, and the intent of this work was, according to the author's own preface, "to attempt a story in the bygone style of Mrs. Radcliffe."[56] Unless one wishes to label *The Mysteries of Udolpho* picaresque, instead of Gothic, there is little basis for so regarding the imitation. Chandler takes the presence of gypsies, and Turpin's pre-criminal exploits as signs of the pícaro,[57] but this is scarcely defensible.

It is quite true that *Rookwood* contains some seventeen ballads which may be regarded as picaresque in spirit, but they do not alter the essentially criminal orientation of the book. No more does the description of the hero in *Jack Sheppard:* "Taken altogether, his psyoignomy [sic] resembled one of those vagabond heads which Murillo delighted to paint, and for which Guzman d'Alfarache, Lazarillo de Tormes or Estevanillo Gonzales might have sat"[58] or John Gay's alleged comment that Jack's adventures "would be quite as entertaining as the histories of Guzman d'Alfarache, Lazarillo de Tormes, Estevanillo Gonzales, Meriton Latroon, or any of my favorite rogues—and far more instructive."[59] The very fact that Jack Sheppard is grouped by Ainsworth with the others is his list of evidence that the author never really grasped the essential differences between felon and pícaro. Jack is devoid of genuine humor, his exploits are brutal, and his attitude morbid and undeserving of sympathy. In short, the book is no more picaresque than *Rookwood* and cataloguing a few assorted pícaros does not make it so.

On the other hand, Charles Dickens was influenced by numerous picaresque personalities, since he was surely aware of every type of individual in London, and this, in addition to his wide and omnivorous reading, would have given him an understanding of unfortunate youth which not even the *Siglo de Oro* authors could have bettered.

Dickens was especially fascinated by the cockneys, whose vocabulary and attitude toward life are startingly reminiscent of the *novela,* especially such works as Cervantes' *Rinconete y Cortadillo.*[60] Dickens' writing was greatly influenced by his sense of visual detail, and his cartoon illustrations were equalled only by the description in words which accompanied them. It has often been remarked that either would have conveyed the image, so it is no wonder that the combination was irresistible.

The outstanding picaresque cockney of his works was, beyond a doubt, Sam Weller of *The Pickwick Papers.* Although Mr. Pickwick's servant is very much in the possession of a father, it is that worthy himself who defines the picaresque nature of his son's upbringing when he states:

> I took a great deal o' pains with his eddication, sir; let him run in the streets when he was wery young, and shift for his-self. It's the only way to make a boy sharp.[61]

With the exception of Alfred Jingle, professional villain rather than rogue, Sam is perhaps the only level-headed major character in the book, and his firm grasp of reality again defines the pícaro, who had no time for fantasies or ideals. There can be little doubt that Sam is the distillation of many cockneys whom Dickens observed in London, but Sam's personality is the same one which Aristophanes labeled Xanthias, and which Lazarillo so completely exemplifies.

It is, however, in the autobiographical *David Copperfield* that the true picaresque novel again appears in England, for here the pattern is shown with a remarkable fidelity to the Spanish prototype.

The young David has parents at the start of the story, it is true, but within the first 180 pages of the book both are taken away from him, and from that point forward the world becomes a totally hostile place. During his period of employment in Murdstone and Grinby's warehouse, David is thrown upon his own resources, and has to depend upon his wits in dealing with his struggle for existence. He comments bitterly, both on his own behalf and the author's that "I know enough of the world now, to have lost the capacity of being much surprised by anything, but it is a matter of some surprise to me, even now, that I can have been so easily thrown away at such an age." Charles Dickens' father, whom the author used to visit in prison during this period in real life, becomes Mr. Micawber in the novel, and David is exposed to some of the same bitter realities which other pícaros learned at such an early age.

Since the tale is told by Dickens, it is sentimentalized and, as Cross points out, in this author sentimentalism is simply a phase of his idealism. This particular aspect of his writing often has the effect of destroying a certain amount of what would otherwise be horribly naturalistic description, but the realism, at least, survives to a marked degree.

Realism is the keynote of *Oliver Twist,* but in no sense is this work believable as a picaresque tale. It is a fairy tale from the very start, with utterly evil and divinely good characters. If the heuristic and allegorical society were not sufficient to destroy the atmosphere created by realistic descriptions, Oliver himself finishes the job with his impossible lines. Dickens commented in the preface of his book that "I saw no reason, when I wrote this book, why the dregs of life...should not serve the purpose of a moral," but the most imaginative reader could hardly picture a Lazarillo pleading "Oh! Pray have mercy on me and do not make me steal. For the love of all the Bright Angels that rest in Heaven, have mercy upon me"! Dickens was under no obligation to create a pícaro, and he did not do so.

It would, therefore, be a serious error to imply that Dickens, as a writer, was in the picaresque tradition. The more accurate evaluation appears to be that he was one of the ultra-Victorians, and restricted himself to highly didactic, highly proper stories which emphasized the already popular social satire and criticism of the day. The irony is that his own life involved a genuine picaresque element, and it is mainly in his autobiographical novel that this aspect appears.

Like Dickens, William Makepeace Thackeray learned the trade of writing as a journalist, and many of his characters seem to reflect the personalities encountered in his earlier experiences and writings. This has, in fact, been regarded by some critics as the basic flaw in his writing, since it tended to keep him from developing a strong central narrative in his novels.

Whether it is a flaw or not, what has been pointed out in Smollett's style[62] is here equally applicable, and becomes a point of evidence in establishing the character of Becky Sharp in *Vanity Fair* (1847) as the Justina *à Là Inglesa.* She is portrayed as the beautiful and totally immoral offspring of a ne'er-do-well French dancing master, determined to make her way in the world with the help of her body and her wits, both of which were amply qualified for the job.

Chandler, for some inexplicable reason, refers to her as "perfectly passionless,"[63] from which one is tempted to assume that he never read the book. The reader is told by

Thackeray that Becky's face "had before worn an almost livid look of hatred"[64]: ' "Are you all here to insult me?' cried Becky in a fury"[65]; and finally, ' "Couldn't forget *him*!' cried out Becky 'that selfish humbug, that low-bred Cockney dandy, that padded booby.' "[66] It would indeed be hard to imagine her in a passion, if the above remarks do not so qualify.

Chandler's encomium of Becky as the ultra-pícara is not justified, in the opinion of this writer. The woman is, beyond a doubt, utterly heartless and immoral, but there is one essential point in which she is disqualified for the crown, and that the most important one—she loses!

Despite her beauty, her intelligence, her wits, and her many social talents, Becky Sharp ends as a derelict slut in a London slum, lower even than she began, and without a sign of the many benefits she once claimed. This is in direct contradiction to the picaresque hero of either sex who, by definition, wins the battle against life. Thackeray, much in the style of Dickens, lines up his cast on stage at the end of the play and distributes blessings and punishments as he thinks his readers will see fit, and what Becky receives, as attested by Thackeray's own illustration, is utter failure.

Thackeray's genuine interest in writing the story was not Becky or any other person, but rather "Vanity Fair" itself, and the style of living which it creates and demands. It has been shown that the English Victorian novel, however picaresque, displayed a didacticism which demanded certain conventions, and one of these is a "crime does not pay" ending. Becky is, therefore, the morally Anglicized pícara who lives the life, but does not win out at the end of it.

Although Dickens dipped into the rather strong waters of *picarismo* quite unintentionally, and Thackeray was more interested in a society than any single individual in it, there can be no question that Charles Lever knew exactly what he was doing. In 1849 he produced *Confessions of Con Cregan,* labeling the hero, on the title page, "The Irish Gil Blas." The description is apt, and the adventures justify what might otherwise be simply an Irish exaggeration. Perhaps the author's genuine understanding of the picaresque tradition is best expressed by his hero, when the latter muses:

> Many years afterwards, in the checkered page of my existence, when I have sat at lordly tables and listened to the sharpened wit and polished raillery of the highborn and the gifted, my mind has often reverted to that beggar horde, and thought how readily the cutting jest was answered, how soon repartee followed attack— what quaint fancies, what droll conceit, passed through those brains, where one could have deemed there was no room for aught save brooding guilt and sad repining.

This is indeed the saving grace of the pícaro through the ages—the ability to see the wry humor in a life which would otherwise be too deadly earnest to bear. Charles Lever combined a native Irish wit with a novelist's imagination to produce a pícaro worthy of Lazarillo himself.

Another intentionally picaresque work was Augustus Mahew's *Paved with Gold,* which appeared in 1857. There is none of the initial exposure to good breeding or eventual redemption through a loving aunt which Dickens introduced in *David Copperfield:* in fact, although the picaresque background is carefully constructed, Mahew based most of his descriptions upon actual observations. The young protagonist Phillip Merton is born in a prison, nursed in a workhouse, and knows no schooling other than that provided for paupers. He runs away from school to join the street arabs of London, tries a multitude of occupations, all moderately dishonest, and eventually becomes a criminal. With his father, Vautrin, he ceases to be a pícaro in all but a few incidents, and permanently crosses the line into felony.

In the remaining years of the nineteenth century there were many adventure novels produced, almost all of which included roguish characters of some description. Writers such as Charles Kingsley, Wilkie Collins, Charles Reade, and countless others dealt with the question of the unfortunate individual in competition with the rest of the world, and their heroes often exhibited characteristics which were also native to the pícaro. This was, however, merely a natural similarity, and in almost no case was there any evidence of direct indebtedness to the Spanish originals, or any intention on the part of the author to emulate, or to copy them.

The western world was becoming socially conscious, and with increasing efficiency was reducing the problem to a simple dichotomy of obedience to the law, or criminality. The pícaro, like any other untamed animal at large, began to have more and more difficulty in finding a place to hide.

Eventually, he will find none.

9

The Pícaro in
the United States

The historical periods discussed in preceding chapters have all been distinguished by societies which were either at or past their peaks and, in a few cases, already far down the other side toward decay. Perhaps the best example of this is the *Siglo de Oro* itself, since in the Spain of Lazarillo's time only memories of greatness remained. The present was sordid and unproductive of new ideas or vigor.

Although we are still too close to the subsequent centuries, and their relative stages of development in France, Germany and England, to evaluate them as accurately as we can Spain and Rome, it is quite evident that such a stage did not arrive in the United States of America prior to the 20th century. This is not meant to imply, at least at this point, that any sort of a peak did appear then—it means only that a careful investigation will reveal that during the historical period prior to approximately 1900, America was on a healthy upgrade social development.[1]

There are several conditions prerequisite to the creation and continued existence of a pícaro, and a detailed review of them is essential to determine the suitability of America as a picaresque background.

The first inescapable requirement is a comparatively crowded, or at least well-settled area, in which a beggar or a stray boy would not be too obvious. Seville, in 1613, was a busy metropolis, and supported a criminal class into which Cervantes' Rinconete and Cortadillo[2] fitted easily, once they had made the necessary professional contacts. Two more thieves made little difference to the general public, and there was no particular reason to notice them, until they were caught.

On the other hand two men could not possibly have moved into a small village, anywhere, without arousing notice and comment, and being forced in one way or another to identify themselves. As strangers and recent arrivals they would have been subject to increased observation and comment, if not actual suspicion. This is the reason that 18th century London was such a wonderful breeding place for the picaresque and criminal types, and why there was, comparatively, less crime in the sparser populated rural areas. (It may be noted that this is still quite true, not only in England, but in almost any modern country.)

A second prerequisite condition for *picarismo* was the casual, general acceptance of hunger and poverty. The simplest way of realizing this is to visualize a tramp, first in a "hobo jungle" and then at a Park Avenue reception. While both groups are quite aware of poverty from an intellectual standpoint, into only the former society could the tramp move with comparative ease.

The unknown author of *Lazarillo de Tormes* depended upon his readers' realizing that a blind beggar and his ragged boy would simply go unnoticed in a Spanish town, even perhaps by those from whom they begged. They were, so to speak, a part of the normal scenery of the country.

Much of the same situation existed in 20th century wartime Italy and China, when literally thousands of children were turned loose to fend for themselves when their parents were killed or lost. The residents of the larger metropolitan areas, such as Rome or Hong Kong, simply became accustomed to unattached waifs in the streets, and normally paid no attention at all to a few more or less. In the same way, the pícaro was left to his own devices only if he were one of so many that he could benefit (?) from the general disinterestedness. In any society which considered the individual, and took responsibility for his welfare, the stray boy would be made a subject of general interest, and his future life and development would be forced into the socially acceptable grooves already prepared. It would, normally, be only a matter of time until he identified with the community, and ceased to differ in outlook from those who were responsible for his socialization. This, it may be noted, was what Aunt Polly had in mind for Huckleberry Finn, and one of the points in that story is that his specific refusal to be subjected to the socialization process of either Aunt Polly or Huck's father was the reason for the river voyage.

The third requisite condition, and one which will apply directly to America, is that there must be a surplus of human beings in the society before its members are willing to sacrifice one, or even permit him to be casually non-productive.

It has been pointed out that one of the characteristics of a decadent society is the surplus of people for whom the State has no particular use except in time of war. When the final expulsion of the Moors was accomplished in 1492, when the Wars of the Roses ended (or perhaps at Mary Tudor's death in 1588), and when peace was at last declared in America in 1783, Spain, England and the Colonies each began a period of peace, but with entirely different results.

Spain had used up much of its wealth and internal resources, and the expulsion of the Jews and Moors had deprived the nation of some of its most energetic and valuable citizens, for whom replacements were simply not available. Spain's period of peace was, therefore, marked not by prosperity or progress, but rather by lethargy and hardship, as has been discussed above.[3] The inevitable result was that Spain's opportunity was consumed in the simple effort to survive, and as a consequence there was almost literally no social progress.

On the other hand, England, under Elizabeth, entered a period of unquestionable prosperity. A vigorous, wholesome atmosphere prevailed in the underpopulated, agricultural country, and a highly organized social structure provided a place for every legitimate citizen, thereby insuring both his security and behavior. Only in the larger metropolitan areas, such as London, was there to be found a class of people who did not identify with the general welfare. (There were, of course, the inevitable vagrants in rural areas. But such persons were, by their very disassociation with society, so assiduously persecuted, however, that their lives must have resembled a fox hunt—from the point of view of the fox!)

The third in this post-conflict comparison, America, exemplifies a still greater positive effort, since the country consisted of a comparatively insignificant number of settlers along the fringes of an incredibly vast wilderness. Land was quite literally available for the taking, and it was the people to settle it which constituted the principal problem. In 1790 the population of the United States was less than 4,000,000,[4] of whom 95% lived east of the Alleghany mountains.[5] As a result, a man was a far greater asset than an acre.

The arrival of a stranger in an early American community was an event, and the individual was granted the closest attention and the greatest interest, such as might be at an isolated western ranch today. While the Colonal visitor might not be suspect, depending upon his appearance, and the attitude of the local residents, his clothes, horse, weapons, speech and declared reasons for being there would receive the closest attention of the entire populace.

Hospitality on the frontier has always been regarded as an inescapable and, in many cases, a well-nigh sacred obligation, so that the stranger might expect to be housed, fed and, if necessary, cared for in illness by the community at large. Under no circumstances would he be permitted to remain hungry or ill while the community went about its normal business and ignored his needs.

Finally, unless he were clearly a traveller who must continue on his way after a night's lodging, or a man with inescapable attachments to another area, a unified effort would probably be made to persuade him to settle in the area. There was no organized military or police protection available in most communities, and there was always a dearth of skilled craftsmen, so almost any man capable of productive work and bearing arms was a valuable potential addition to the community, and the infrequent opportunities for acquiring new men members were too rare to be overlooked.

This, then, was the basic situation in Colonial America, with regard to any white man. Where could there be room for Lazarillo?

Although poverty and excessive population were so clearly not the problem in America which they had been in Europe, there were still asocial individuals who so completely exemplified the independent, resistant-to-rules American that their lives and behavior were essentially picaresque.

It has been shown that Xanthias exhibited certain elements of behavior which were also present in Guzmán de Alfarache, as well as Roderick Random and Meriton Latroon. None of these literary personalities were in any sense carbon copies, or even a combination of their predecessors. Each was, instead, a topical adaptation of the fundamental *picarismo* which existed regardless of geography and century. Slave or freeman, bastard or legitimate, educated or ignorant, the pícaro continued to survive in real life, and in American literature as well.

Charles Brockden Brown was probably the first American to earn a living by his writings, and so it is perhaps not unsuitable that he should be the first to produce an American novel with distinct picaresque elements. Although there is a far stronger emphasis on the Gothic, *Arthur Mervyn or Memoirs of the Year 1793* can be related clearly to the picaresque novel, albeit via eighteenth century English works such as *Joseph Andrews* and *Roderick Random.* Brown was an educated man, but we have no evidence that his work is related directly to the *Siglo de Oro;* the indebtedness to Fielding and Smollett is, however, unmistakable.

Their descriptions of the minutiae of everyday life in

England contribute a realism to their books which has always been a characteristic of the picaresque novel, and Brown almost bettered them in this particular. Thomas Wentworth Higginson is quoted as declaring:

> With all his inflation of style, he was undoubtedly, in his way, a careful observer. The proof of that is, that he has preserved for us many minor points of life and manner which make the Philadelphia of a century ago now more familiar to us than is any other American city of that period.[6]

The principal obstruction to consideration of Arthur Mervyn as a pícaro is his naïveté and innocence. Yet this is not an impossible combination, since the lack of sophistication is so fundamentally characteristic of the early American literary character, with the exception of sneering villains such as Brown's Welbeck, that it must not be granted too much weight in the consideration of any specific case.

There is, in *Arthur Mervyn,* a clearly defined movement from ignorance to a knowledge of the world. Darrel Abel points out that this will be true of such successive protagonists as Melville's Redburn, Mark Twain's Huckleberry Finn, and James' Christopher Newman, and like them, Arthur Mervyn "comes through the experience with a tempered and compassionate morality that is better than his original naïve innocence."[7] This same painful process is quite evident in *Lazarillo de Tormes,* as well as countless other novels which followed in that path, although Charles Brockden Brown's almost intolerable moralizing succeeded in disguising the basic direction. It requires a determined tolerance to accept such scenes as that in which Arthur is shot by an overexcited young woman, and, amid the blood (his) and the tears (hers), exclaims didactically:

> I hope that you will derive instruction from the event. Your rashness had like to have sacrificed the life of one who is your friend, and to have exposed yourself to infamy and death, or, at least, to the pangs of eternal remorse. Learn, from hence, to curb your passions, and especially to keep at a distance from every

murderous weapon, on occasions when rage is likely to take the place of reason.

The moral, if not the credibility, is beyond question.

Arthur Mervyn served to set the first pattern of the American novel, and while it is poor writing, it is highly representative of the degree to which there are identifiable picaresque elements in American thought of that period. For this reason, if no other, it deserves a place in the picaresque tradition.

Perhaps the most directly picaresque work of the period was Hugh Henry Brackenridge's *Modern Chivalry* (1792-1815), since it is picaresque in tone, in characterization, and in the author's expressed intent as well. Although the novel was based upon Brackenridge's own Hudibrastic poem "The Modern Chevalier," a sort of pilot study for the longer prose work, the direct use of his previously published material is limited to the first two books of *Modern Chivalry.*

The story of Captain Farrago and his servant Teague O'Regan is based upon the relationship between these two, and it is clearly related to the Don Quijote/Sancho Panza format, although with somewhat less emphasis on the servant's peasant wisdom. In this case, it is the servant's increased opportunities in a new, raw civilization which receive a great deal of the reader's attention. Fred Lewis Pattee draws this conclusion somewhat effusively when he asserts:

> In *Modern Chivalry* we have two contrasted ideals—the conservative East, embodied in the wise Captain Farrago with his caution, his store of parallel cases drawn often from erudite volumes, his cool common sense; and opposed to him we have the new West, vibrant with physical life, irresistible, extravagant, unconventional, seemingly immoral, wholly uncultured, independent even to license, embodied in the red-headed Irish bogtrotter, Teague O'Regan. And of the two, Teague alone is alive.[9]

In the opinion of this writer, describing Captain Farrago as "wise" indicates a lack of understanding of Brackenridge's underlying satire, since Farrago is a pedant and, on occasion, a fool. The contrast between the two men, however, is most accurately described.

The critical consensus that the picaresque element is clear, and the indebtedness apparent, is most interesting, since such universal agreement is to be found in reference to almost no other American story. For example, Abernathy comments that "This excellent political satire reflects the influence of Cervantes, Fielding, and Sterne,"[10] Cairns describes the work as "a rambling prose burlesque showing the influence of Don Quixote in the plan, and of Smollett, Sterne and Fielding in the manner,"[11] Pattee declares that "it suggests Scarron's *Roman Comique* and Le Sage's *Gil Blas,*"[12] Lewisohn labels the story "picaresque and satiric,"[13] and Abel flatly defines Farrago as a "back-country American Quixote."[14] If one may assume that these are all original opinions, reached independently after a study of the novel, then the consensus is indeed impressive.

Brackenridge himself denied any satirical or political intent, and in fact claimed that he had resisted the urging of friends that he use his book for such a purpose:

> Indeed, as it has been known that I was engaged in writing something, persons who either took, or pretended to take, some interest in my affairs, have urged me very much to depart a little from my usual way, and make a little irony, by way of seasoning the composition.[15]

He refused, he continues, because he is not in the habit of looking for irony in human affairs, and therefore there is no intentional irony in his book. Whether this is his true lack of understanding of his own work (a dubious assumption, surely), or whether it is the type of thing he might have felt Sterne would say, cannot be determined. The irony is there, however, it is deftly done, and it really matters little to this discussion whether it was intentional or not.

The significance of *Modern Chivalry,* and its position in this study is therefore obvious: it shows beyond question that not only *picarismo* but a conscious indebtedness had crossed the Atlantic, and that there was a direct applicability to the American colonial scene.

During the twenty-three year period when Brackenridge was producing his novel, there was a most interesting indebtedness expressed, not only to the *Siglo de Oro,* but to indebted English authors as well. In 1803 Tabitha Tenney produced *Female Quixotism: Exhibited in the Romantic Opinions and Extravagant Adventures of Dorcasina Sheldon.* This story was intended to strike a death blow at the romantic novel, which the lady considered a serious threat to morality of young ladies, whom she hoped to assist in avoiding romantic pitfalls. It was therefore dedicated "to all Columbian Young Ladies Who read Novels and Romances," and took for its heroine a plain country girl, saturated with tales of romantic adventure.

The model for Mrs. Tenney's story, in addition to the durable Don Quijote, was unquestionably the *Female Quixote,* published by Mrs. Lennox some fifty-one years earlier.[16] The parody may have been effective as preventative propaganda, but it has not survived as literature.

There was, in fact, almost no significant work of long fiction after *Modern Chivalry* until James Fenimore Cooper accepted his wife's challenge, and began writing novels with the expressed intent of bettering Jane Austen's *Persuasion.* Whether he made good his boast or not, they constitute the next major American works of literature. Of especial interest to this discussion are the "Leatherstocking Tales," and *The Pioneers* in particular.

Although Arthur Mervyn was unquestionably a home-grown product of rural Pennsylvania, Natty Bumpo is the first American *Naturmensch*—the almost legendary type who will be Longknife, Deerslayer, Kit Carson, Daniel Boone and a whole bookful of John Myers Myers' heroes. For this reason, he must be considered in relationship to *picarismo,* and our conclusions concerning him will apply to his entire literary succession.

Natty clearly meets the physical requirements of Lazarillo, since Cooper took care to make his hero of a lower social level (in fact, the finding of a suitable mate, neither too high nor too low, was one of the writer's greatest subsequent problems), and he is without any other resources than his own wits and physical strength. True, he is offered the opportunity to live on the bounty of the Temples and Effinghams, but Cooper has taken care to create a character who would be unwilling to do this.

The society which fines, stocks and imprisons Natty is certainly hostile, and one whose laws he does not hesitate to defy for his own purposes. It is, in fact, his refusal to submit to the rules and mores of the society in which he now lives, which causes his downfall, since he is unable to resist its organized strength.

Ludwig Bemelmans deals with the Bavarian counterpart of Cooper's hero as the type with "moss in his boots and roots hanging out of his ears,"[17] and the description applies to our American domestic variety equally well. The difference is that *Rübezahl* comes into contact only with the simple German peasants, who are quite willing to accept him at his face value, and Natty Bumpo is forced to deal with Judge Temple's sophistry and Elizabeth's wiles.

Natty is, in fact, just too naïve for the world in which he finds himself living, and this problem is to follow him through the annals of American literary history. Exemplifying the ideals of knighthood, albeit with a coonskin cap and faulty grammar, he is unprepared to deal with a constantly changing society, and his only resource will always be physical flight from civilization to a never-never land beyond the frontier.

By definition, then, Natty must forever lose his battle to exist in a hostile society and he is, therefore, never a pícaro.

That he may be regarded with some justification as the first of the anti-heroes is a matter which will be discussed in a subsequent chapter.

Another author whose adventure stories cannot be regarded as picaresque is Herman Melville, and the reason is much the same. Instead of the unhesitating rescality of such sea-going rogues as Roderick Random, Melville's Wellingborough Redburn exhibits a sort of whining piety, which is not only a complete contrast to the self-sufficient pícaro, but which shows how ill-equipped the American youth is to fight his own battles. *Redburn* is a fascinating story, since it is Melville talking about his own youthful adventures, but it is just that—adventure, not *picarismo.*

The American pícaro really made his first appearance in Mark Twain's works, probably because this was one of the first American authors who had grown up among the people and situations which he portrays. Just as the best picaresque English novels had been the result of personal experience (Dickens as a waif in London, Fielding as a police court magistrate, etc.), Mark Twain's observations of life along the Mississippi gave him a wealth of incident and characters to draw upon, and one which he never really exhausted.

The comparatively autobiographical *Tom Sawyer* exhibited certain picaresque elements, principally involving resistance to rules and mores. Nevertheless, Tom is in a secure position, since he has a home, and his adventures and perils are all voluntary. In other words, his basic position is not picaresque. Injun Joe is really none of Tom's business, and the adventure in the cave with Becky is actually more likely to happen on a Sunday School picnic than to a boy searching for enough food and shelter to stay alive. Between incidents, Tom always returns to Aunt Polly to be scolded, washed, and otherwise mothered. The puppy who crawls under the fence once in a while, and then scurries back to his master, cannot be regarded as a stray dog.

This is hardly the case with Huckleberry Finn, however.

Although he is nominally in the same position as Tom, he actually regards it as a temporary, expedient arrangement, tolerable only because it is better than living with his father. Huck never really identifies with Aunt Polly's household, and the reader is kept aware that it is only a matter of time before he will leave.

Although the relationship of "Pap" to Huck is technically paternal, there is really no emotional involvement, and a closer analogy is provided by Lazarillo and his beggar. Huck does not choose to stay with his father because he realizes (a very hard, practical picaresque realization, indeed) that his situation is not only insecure but actually dangerous, in view of the old man's drinking and delirium tremens, and the boy does not hesitate to fool his father in order to escape.

Once Huck and Nigger Jim start on their voyage down the Mississippi, the picaresque format is complete. Huck is being sought by his father, Aunt Polly, Judge Thatcher, and other assorted people, including those who want the escaping slave too. At almost every stage of their trip they encounter hostility of some sort, well-larded with the actual physical dangers of snakes, family feuds, and steamboat collisions. They have no weapons or money, and are dependent solely upon their wits for survival, in a very definitely hostile environment.

The structure of the novel immediately suggests the picaresque works of both the *Siglo de Oro* and the eighteenth century English adventure tales, since it is outrightly episodic, commencing immediately in Chapter I. The river, always present in the reader's thoughts, provides a continuity which renders a more specifically structural continuum necessary. Just as one understands that the pícaro must continue moving from one master to another, from one place to another, so it is obvious that the river is carrying Huck and Jim from one adventurous episode to the next.

Huckleberry Finn is told in the first person, after the adventures have been completed, which is a normal pattern of the picaresque novel, and the ending is satisfactory to the protagonist. As always, Mark Twain had a target in mind, in this case the misconception that wisdom and goodness come only from education and social position; this same criticism can be found three hundred years earlier in Cervantes' gentle satires. Mark Twain was most conscious of this, as he proves over and over again in such works as *A Connecticut Yankee in King Arthur's Court*(1899). It has been shown that there has been a steady trickle of such works since *Don Quijote,* and this is one of them.

In the opinion of this writer, Mark Twain set out to write a picaresque novel in the classic tradition, placed in the American scene which he know best, just as a craftsman might, in China, carve a set of Chinese figures for chessmen, rather than the more traditional but less familiar Persian shahs and elephants. The almost endless discussions of symbolism in *The Adventures of Huckleberry Finn* have ignored this aspect. There has been, at best, a certain casual, almost grudging acknowledgement, such as Sculley Bradley's "This 'picaresque' element was prominent in the burlesque romances, such as *Don Quixote* and *Gil Blas,* which inspired Mark Twain, in this book and elsewhere, in making his attack on the shams of romantic chivalry,"[18] but mention of indebtedness itself has been slighted.

With no expressed intention to relate this work to the picaresque, Leslie A. Fiedler has done so to a degree which is truly impressive, in view of the defined criteria which this study has adopted:

> *Huckleberry Finn* is, then, essentially a book about a marginal American type, who only wants to stay alive; but who does not find this very easy to do, being assailed on the one side by forces of violence which begrudge him the little he asks, and on the other by forces of benevolence which insist that he ask for more. Against this modesty and singleness of his purpose, everything else is measured and weighed: religion, the social order, other men. Huck exists on a sub-moral level; for he cannot afford the luxury of living by the moral codes of the Widow Douglases of his

small-town world. Such codes assume a standard of security, if not actual prosperity, to which he does not even aspire.[19]

Omit the proper nouns, and this defines exactly Lazarillo de Tormes' position in sixteenth century Spain.

Others of Mark Twain's works exhibit picaresque elements, as has been noted, but these appear to be the result of his native tendency to ridicule stuffiness and outworn tradition. It is only in *Huckleberry Finn* that there appears to have been a conscious effort to write an American picaresque novel.

Why this same effect is not present in the writings of William Dean Howells is really a problem. The man was unquestionably influenced by Spanish works, as he himself remarks in *My Literary Passions:*

> I read Longfellow's Spanish Student...and I instantly conceived for it the passion which all things Spanish inspired in me... The hero's rogue servant Chispa seemed to me, then and long afterward, so fine a bit of Spanish character that I chose his name for my first pseudonym when I began to write.[20]

This is an interesting confession, since Chispa is the complete and unquestionable pícaro, in the exact sense of Lazarillo. He is the shrewd servant of a minor Spanish nobleman, and is the means of that worthy's dishonest and abortive efforts to make love to the gypsy dancer. Chispa's sayings, his resignation to success and failure alike, and the very words he chooses are in the generic tradition of the *Siglo de Oro:*

> Abernuncio Satanas! and a plague on all lovers who ramble about at night drinking the elements, instead of sleeping quietly in their beds. Every dead man to his cemetery, say I; and every friar to his monastery. Now, here's my master Victorian, yesterday a cow keeper, and today a gentleman; yesterday a student, and today a lover; and I must be up later than the nightingale, for as the abbot sings, so must the sacristan respond. God grant that he may soon be married, for then shall all this serenading cease.[21]

Although "The Spanish Student" may have been a youthful enthusiasm, Howells was fifty-eight years old when he wrote *My Literary Passions,* and he included not only a chapter on Longfellow's poetic drama, but a separate one on *Lazarillo de Tormes* as well. It is in this that he indicates his personal indebtedness to, and approval of, the Spanish model:

> I do not know that I should counsel others to do so, or that the general reader would find his account in it, but I am sure that the intending author of American fiction would do well to study the Spanish picaresque novels; for in their simplicity of design he will find one of the best forms for an American story.22

In view of these commitments to the literary merits of *picarismo,* spanning virtually his whole life, it seems incredible that, in a canon which includes forty full-length novels, there is not one which is actually picaresque in nature.

In *The Rise of Silas Lapham* Howells might easily have presented a pícaro, if he had so desired, since the story involves a "flashback" and the present character of the protagonist is therefore not necessarily the same as in the story he relates. This opportunity was quickly discarded, however, since the author almost immediately defines his hero's childhood as "sweetened, however, by the recollections of a devoted mother, and a father who...was no less ambitious for the advancement of his children."23 With such a beginning, *picarismo* is impossible.

In fact, until the highly naturalistic stories of Dreiser and Norris made their appearance, the picaresque disappeared almost entirely from the American literary scene, and a Victorian didacticism took hold of the novel, due in part to the influence of such American writers as Henry James, and in part to the English moral tales which had replaced Lever, Mahew and Dickens. The Horatio Alger hero was much more acceptable in America than Lazarillo, and it was virtuous suffering which was most admired.

America was booming, and with increasing industrialization came increasing opportunities for employment and material success. True, such opportunities frequently involved pitifully sub-standard working conditions, but this did not alter the fact that it was unnecessary to starve. A particular social apex was about to be reached in America and, as in the period of the Spanish picaresque authors, the downgrade from this peak would again provide a fertile field for social misfits—including the pícaro.

10

The Pícaro

in Latin America

Before considering the picaresque element in 20th century writings, it is necessary to realize that a simultaneous literary development was proceeding in Latin America during the period of English and French colonization in the more northerly latitudes. The literatures which developed in those countries settled by English colonists were entirely different from the Spanish, once the initial period of chronicles was passed. To understand this, it is instructive to examine the comparative conditions of life in Spain and England beginning about the 16th century, since these conditions determined the future courses of their respective colonies.

One characteristic condition of colonization is that the first social and religious orientations of the colony are precisely those of the parent nation. Even when the purpose of separation is to effect a change in one aspect of behavior, such as the Pilgrims contemplated, the basic human relationship remains that of parent and offspring, rather than enemies. The North American colonists continued, in fact, to regard themselves essentially as patriotic and abused Englishmen until the actual gunfire of the Revolutionary War was heard.

It is worth noting that, even during a period of bitter warfare, and despite the inevitable barrage of propaganda, American colonists continued to read the 18th century

English authors of novels and poetry. After independence was achieved, American writers patterned their work upon the best English models. The conflict was, after all, political—not artistic.

If a literary relationship is thus able to survive a war of independence, and considerable verbal abuse, how much more binding must it be when the geographical separation is reluctant and cooperative? There was great reason for English colonists to seek total separation from England; there was none whatsoever for Spaniards to shun their centuries-old heritage. It is certainly not surprising, then, that the earlier Spanish writings in the New World were consciously imitative of their familiar and beloved Peninsular prototypes.

The *conquistadores* who came west across the ocean from Spain were products of an anachronistic culture which had never discarded the medieval concepts now becoming obsolete in the rest of Europe. Italy had begun the new respect for human values which we have, perhaps incorrectly, regarded as a rebirth rather than a reevaluation, the tide of the Renaissance had moved northward triumphantly, but Spain stood aside in dour silence, and watched it pass. Perhaps it was pride, perhaps the Inquisition, perhaps the fundamental matter of seven centuries of unremitting war, instead of an occasional and glamorous jaunt to the Holy Land—but there was no Renaissance in Spain. Instead, and to the general dissatisfaction of the people, their rigidly structured society settled even more implacably into the inflexible mold of *hidalgo* and commoner.

The initial difference was not so important to the commoner, as the permanence of the disadvantage. To be born poor in Spain meant a shortened life of hardship and disease, with no hope for betterment except the rather unconvincing prospect of Heaven at the end.

Consider, however, the situation of a common Spanish soldier or colonist in Spanish America! The very fact that he was a Peninsular Spaniard, regardless of his parentage, made him a member of a privileged class in the New World. Instead of being merely a beggar's son, a bastard offspring of some peasant girl, or one of the countless gutter brats in Seville, he was a charter member of the conquering national group, who could look down upon every Indian, every Negro, and every man of whatever origin who could not say that he was born in Spain. And furthermore, to his incredulous delight and gratification, the traditional dichotomy which separated officer and common soldier was far less important in *El Nuevo Mundo* than their common Spanish citizenship. The poorest of the poor, so long as he came from Spain, found himself to be, by right of birth, a member of the most privileged class in all Spanish America.

Under these conditions there would be no discontented and downtrodden class of Spanish colonist, such as might include the pícaro, since every Spaniard was now endowed with a prestige beyond his wildest dreams. *Picarismo* requires helpless outcasts and a class of downtrodden poor, and among the Spanish settlers these simply did not exist. The obvious and correct conclusion is that it is fatuous to seek picaresque literature in the early Colonial period.

No society can remain for long in its initial condition, however, and it is to be expected that the inevitable adjustments and liaisons inherent in the colonization process should cause restructuring. All that was required in the new Spanish colonies was sufficient time to breed new generations which lacked the advantages of being born in the parent country.

The Spaniards in Latin America began, inevitably, to produce (with the enthusiastic aid of Indian girls) a new social group of mixed blood, which we call *mestizos.* Of course, the Church and judiciary attempted dutifully to prevent these matings, but no legal code has ever managed to prevent entirely the fusion of conquered and conquering races. All that could be accomplished was to create a set of official social prejudices, which warned the Spaniard that he need look for no approval of his illegitimate children. Perhaps even more important, the laws shortly forbade the competition of half-native offspring with those born of undiluted Spanish blood.

Once this situation was fully developed, the Iberian and medieval social organization was again in control, and the same attitude of resentment and bitterness which characterized the pícaro in Spain began to appear in the new world.

There was a further complication, resulting from a third social class: the Peninsulars who came to the established colonies after the initial privation and bloodshed of the Conquest was ended. By virtue of their birth and hereditary social position in Spain, these native-born Spaniards expected to assume the advantages won with blood and sacrifice by the *criollo,* or American-born Spaniard. The assumption of rightful superiority by a newly-arrived archbishop, judge, or even viceroy was a bitter pill for the *criollo* to swallow. It not only deprived him of a status which he regarded as particularly his, but, in the true Spanish tradition, negated effort and accomplishment in favor of lineage.

With the arrival of the ecclesiastical, judicial, and social hierarchy, which had always been the social determinant in Spain, cities began to arise in the colonies. Mexico, Lima, and Santo Domingo all became centers of transplanted European sophistication and refinement, which the newly-arrived aristocrats, and the newly-created wealthy families, regarded as the outposts and symbols of civilization in the huge wilderness.

Once the Peninsular nobility reassumed its traditional control, the mere fact of being Spanish was no longer a guarantee of success. To be an untitled, uneducated Spaniard in Spanish America now became exactly what it had always been in Spain. Now the adventurers (and their bastard offspring) found themselves in the same position as the pícaro had been during the *Siglo de Oro.*

Undoubtedly there would have been picaresque novels written in Spanish America during this period, were it not that the printing of books was so rigidly controlled by the Inquisition. The law restricted printing to presses in Spain, and publication was therefore entirely under the control of the church. There was a certain amount of illegal printing in the colonies, of course, but the total is insufficient to define a genre. Since the literary development of Spanish America did not parallel that of Spain, one can say only that the social conditions requisite to future *picarismo* were created during the Colonial period.

The important conclusion to be drawn is that the lack of picaresque novels during the Colonial period was the consequence of censorship, and not a lack of suitable personalities and situations.

In considering the picaresque element in Latin American literature, it is essential to separate the pícaro *per se* from those characteristics by which picaresque literature is traditionally identified. It may not appear logical to assert that a book may be a novel containing extensive *picarismo,* without actually being a picaresque novel, or even containing a pícaro, but this is precisely the characteristic condition of many Latin American works.

One of the best examples of this situation, and also the earliest (1636), is the work of Juan Rodriguez Freile, author of *El carnero.* Freile was born in Santa Fe de Bogotá in 1566, his father was one of the soldiers who helped conquer the country, and his family was therefore well-regarded in colonial society. During a six-year stay in Spain, Freile undoubtedly became familiar with the picaresque literature then current, including *Lazarillo de Tormes* and *Guzmán de Alfarache.* These were available not only in Spain; if Freile had missed reading them, he might easily have obtained them at home since this type of literature had been smuggled into the colonies and was generally available before his death in about 1640.

Freile himself was a farmer, not a professional writer, and although he was reported to be well-educated, he did not attend a university. His work contains numerous quotations, but does not reveal any erudition which could not have been acquired by reading. There are references to mythology, Spanish history, and the Latin classics, it is true, but also to Spanish contemporary literature. This would suggest that Freile's reading was omnivorous, rather than merely scholarly, and that he would have been quite familiar with the picaresque novel.

His only significant work, *El carnero,* is not a novel, however, but rather a collection of stories and gossip about officials in Freile's home city. We have no way of knowing exactly what he meant the title of his book to mean, and there has been extensive scholarly speculation, including references to *El libro de los gatos* (ca. 1400) in which "ram" is used by a wolf masquerading as a monk, in place of "pater noster." A more likely interpretation seems to be the 17th Century slang term used for paupers' graves, into which the dead were thrust without proper ceremonies. Whatever the literal meaning of the title, the intent was clearly disrespectful to authority—just like the contents.

Even though Freile used the customary picaresque author's gambit of disguising his social criticism with endless moralizing, it is noteworthy that the book was not published during the author's lifetime, probably because the Inquisition would have regarded it as immoral and potentially subversive. When the work finally appeared, several centuries later, it found a position in literature rather analogous to Thomas Nashe's *Unfortunate Traveller:* a rich lode of information about customs, language and social behavior, with the accent naturally upon Colombia. Other writers have been mining it ever since.

The nature of the incidents described, including murder, robbery and adultery, cannot be justified by the ostentatious morality of the author's comments, and therefore the book remains a disorganized attack upon the vices of colonial society. There is no pretense at the necessary centralization of character and action demanded by the picaresque novel. There is, in fact, neither a single protagonist nor a specific target.

Castigation of society in the person of an individual representative was effective in Spain, but only because of the traditionally stratified social groups. Lazarillo de Tormes takes service with a beggar, a priest, a squire, a friar, a seller of indulgences, a tambourine painter, a chaplain and a constable, all of whom he criticizes bitterly, but none of whom has a name. Why should any be so identified, when he is not an individual but rather the microcosm of an entire professional or social order? In the colonies, however, Spanish society was still so fluid and indeterminate that the identification of a class by a prototype is not yet possible.

The same comment is applicable to a number of other works produced during this period. Antonio de la Calancha produced the *Crónica moralizadora,* which includes history, science and folklore, but also a bitter disapproval of much human behavior. He is particularly indignant at the airs of the Peninsular Spaniards. As one might deduce, Calancha was a typical *criollo,* and so his respectable position as chronicler of the Order of St. Augustine was insufficient to persuade the Inquisition to allow the printing of his *cronica del convento.*

Hogan comments perceptively that Calancha's contribution to picaresque literature is primarily one of style, rather than a deliberate characteristic of the author.[1] This is one of the reasons that the Peruvian should be regarded as an important author, and perhaps the forerunner of the national esthetic movement. There is no doubt, at least, of Ricardo Palma's direct indebtedness to Calancha, and this alone is sufficient reason for the latter's inclusion in this work.

Bartolome Martínez y Vela, on the other hand, cannot be considered one of the Latin American picaresque writers. His *Anales de la Villa Imperial de Potosí,* although it resembles

Calancha's work to the extent of providing a series of tales based upon colonial scandals, is almost an organized anthology of gossip, all of which refers to a time before Martínez y Vela was born. The result is therefore to be regarded as a history, rather than a novel. The author relates his spicy stories with gusto, chortles, but never comments analytically in the characteristic manner of the pícaro.

It would be possible to add to these examples almost *ad infinitum,* if the purpose of this study were merely to identify picaresque elements in Colonial writings. I have already noted, however, that a significant variant of the 17th century Spanish American books is the frequent presence of *picarismo,* without major redirection or the creation of what may be regarded legitimately as a picaresque novel. It was really not until the following century that a new stage was reached in literature, and that was the result of a social and political upheaval, rather than conscious literary evolution.

During the 18th century, the basic conflict between Peninsular Spaniards and *criollos* continued, since there could be no agreement on the question of whether accomplishment or lineage should be the status-granting factor. It must be made clear, however, that since *mestizos* were excluded completely from the ruling classes the entire problem involved only the white minority in Spanish America. At no time was there any question of admitting Indians, Negroes, or *mestizos* to the more important positions of power and influence.

The most significant literary effort of this period was *El Lazarillo de ciegos caminantes,* despite the fact that the authorship, purpose, place of publication, and date were all deliberately (and quite successfully) confused by the author. Literary hoaxes are always fascinating, and "Concolorcorvo" managed one of the best.

The real author of the book has been shown by José J. Real Díaz, in a genuinely brilliant historical study, to be Don Alonso Carrió de la Vandera.[2] This individual, who was a Peninsular Spaniard, was selected by the Crown in 1771 to reorganize the stage posts between Buenos Aires and Lima. Since he was involved in a running bureaucratic battle with his superior, Don José Antonio de Pandó, the General Administrator of Mails, Carrió de la Vandera decided to use the weapon of public satire, in the form of a book. Obviously, to write such a commentary under his own name would be professional suicide, and so he invented the *persona* of a pureblooded descendant of the Incas, who accompanies the Inspector on his trip, and comments as they go.

An additional red herring used by the ingenious author to conceal his responsibility is the identification of "Concolorcorvo" as Don Calixto Bustamente Carlos Inca, who really lived, and who really was the person identified in the story as a descendant of the Incas. The only difference is that he had nothing to do with writing the book.

The deception continued with the alleged facts of publication. Instead of Gijón, as shown on the title page, the work was really printed in Lima, clandestinely, to avoid the inevitable prohibition of the Inquisition. This original edition also showed 1773 as the date of publication, although it could not have been printed before 1775.

In addition to being ingenious, Carrió was a well-educated man. He uses his erudition freely, with numerous references to Feijóo, Quevedo, Cervantes, and the classics, but it is with the casual and unobtrusive ease of a man who no longer finds it necessary to create an impression. The reader is permitted to enjoy the illusion of a simple, if educated, Indian conversing with a high-ranking Spanish gentleman. In this manner, the author presents both points of view so that they may be contrasted, item by item. It is a simple but most effective technique.

The book is a delightful tale, many of the incidents demonstrate the author's understanding of the people and customs of Peru, but there is not the slightest basis for regarding it as a picaresque novel. Carrió de la Vandera was certainly familiar with the Spanish picaresque works of his own and the preceding century (he even mentions Guzmán de Alfarache and Estebanillo González),3 but he had no intention of merely amusing his readers. His was not even a generalized criticism, but rather a specific attack and a specific argument.

Carrió de la Vandera was convinced that the Indians and, in fact, all people not of pure Spanish blood were of an inferior race and therefore could not but profit by the imposition of European civilization upon their admittedly primitive societies. "Concolorcorvo" even argues with the Inspector on this point, and never loses an opportunity to criticize Indian culture, morals, and behavior. He makes brutally clear his belief that, if a man were not a Peninsular, or at least a *criollo,* he could become at most a well-trained and useful animal, regardless of whether he was *mestizo,* Indian, or Negro.

Assorted Spaniards come in for individual criticism, of course (his fundamental purpose, it must be remembered, was to attack Don José Antonio de Pandó), but the difference is that Spaniards are considered as individuals, and Indians and Negroes only as specimens of a race.

Carrió de la Vandera clearly intended to convince his readers, both American and European, that it would be a grievous error to regard the Indians as merely uneducated. He was determined to establish them as an inferior and permanently subjugated race, which Spain must expect to control and employ without any hope for their eventual emancipation. The author's comments sometimes approach indulgence of innocent customs, such as the acceptance of heathen observances at the time of a Church festival,4 but there is always an overtone of contempt for what he regards coldly as semi-civilized barbarians.

"Concolorcorvo" is occasionally and mildly anticlerical, but this is not a significant feature of his tale. The wealth of certain clergy, the magnificence of an archbishop's table, are almost traditional criticisms of the Church by Spanish writers, and Carrió de la Vandera does no more than follow the pattern in this respect.

Anderson-Imbert has dubbed this book a "travel diary,"[5] which is precisely what it is. To call it picaresque is a blurring of the basic lines which define the genre, and careful analysis readily confirms the difference.

It has been pointed out by other critical writers that the story is told in the first person (Alegría goes so far as to call it *"narración de carácter picaresco"*),[6] that the teller of the tale is a servant, and that he moves from place to place. All of this is quite true, but taken all together it still does not justify classification of the work as picaresque.

On the negative side, the character of the speaker is not developed beyond a short sketch at the beginning and the end, which consists largely of mere physical description. Except for the fact that "Concolorcorvo" is an Indian who looks down on other Indians and admires Spaniards, we really know little about him beyond his size and the color of his hair and skin. *Concolorcorvo,* of course, means *"con color de cuervo,"* and the Inspector comments that his companion might turn pale, but cannot blush.

"Concolorcorvo" is the trusted servant of the Inspector, eats the same food, sleeps in the same houses, and is given considerable authority in making arrangements for the trip. As the servant-companion to an important government official and *hidalgo,* it would be out of the question for the Indian to act according to the principles of *picarismo.*

There is social criticism in the book, to be sure, but it is precisely the reverse of that which characterized the *Siglo de Oro.* "Concolorcorvo" is consistent in his critical disapproval of *mestizos,* Indians, and Negroes, and he praises all things Spanish until even the Inspector revolts against the endless cringing.

It is my belief that most of the misinterpretation of this work has resulted from an erroneous identification of the title with Lazarillo de Tormes, who has always been the generic pícaro in Spanish literature. One student of the subject has suggested that the title of Carrió de la Vandera's book is actually a combination of *El Lazarillo de Tormes* and Timoneda's *Sobremesa y alivio de caminantes,*[7] which would appear to be merely an exercise in etymology. Jacques-Charles Brunet actually classified the book in 1865 as a Spanish novel, assuming apparently that anything including the word *Lazarillo* must be of the Iberian picaresque genre.[8]

Chandler avoided this error, as he has done so many times, and classified the work quite correctly as "simply a guide."[9] The simplicity of the matter may perhaps be debatable, but a guide it certainly is. There is no attempt at a plot or development of a character, and it is of paramount critical importance that the teller of the story, "Concolorcorvo" himself, is exactly the same person at the end as at the beginning of the book.

Since Don Alonso Carrió de la Vandera was educated in Spain, he knew the story and character of Lazarillo, of course, but he was using the term in the dictionary definition of "a boy who guides a blind man,"[10] rather than for literary identification. The remainder of the title *El Lazarillo de ciegos caminantes* endorses this interpretation, and the contents of the work itself are the final evidence.

It is this conclusion which justifies and illustrates Alegría's statement that Hispanic America did not produce novels before the second decade of the 19th century.[11]

The turning point was 1810, when the War of Independence began, and traditional social rigidity collapsed. For the first time in Latin America, the non-white element in society became of political importance. It is quite true that the white *criollos* provided the necessary leadership, but without their hitherto despised followers there could have been no successful revolution. Social prejudices vanished as different classes, city dwellers and farmers, and even slaves and free men combined against the overbearing Spanish hierarchy. Mutinies and revolts became commonplace, and one of the most effective weapons in the hands of the revolutionaries was political satire.

Beginning with complaints about Spanish tradition and rule, the writers of these bitter attacks progressed boldly to topical criticism of their own local administrators and, in order to be heard by as many as possible, they started a campaign of pamphleteering. Miguel Hidalgo, for instance, began a paper called *El Despertador Americano* in 1810, in Mexico; Camillio Enríquez started *La Borora de Chile* in 1812. The most successful of all, however, was *El Pensador Mexicano,* which José Joaquín Fernandez de Lizardi introduced in the same year. This was his first in a long line of periodicals, and the one from which he derived the pen name which he used for the rest of his life.

These topical satires during the period of 1810-1825 led logically into a new form of picaresque literature. All of the satirists and pamphleteers writing during the early decades of the 19th century were familiar with the traditional picaresque novels of the *Siglo de Oro,* and the comparative anarchy created by the destruction of traditional Spanish institutions greatly favored the reappearance of *picarismo.*

It is to the work of Lizardi, after 1812, that we must look for the first (and almost the only) genuine approach to a picaresque novel that would ever be achieved in Hispanic America. Even the resemblance of this book to those of the *Siglo de Oro* has been a matter of almost excessive discussion. The problem is complicated by the understandable circumstance that Lizardi was only vaguely interested in the artistic merit of his works as novels, and therefore his four books varied greatly in their stylistic indebtedness.

The man himself was not a creative writer in the belletristic sense, but rather a political and social propagandist. His original format was the topical poem, sold for a few pennies on the streets of Mexico City, and it is significant that, from the very beginning of his career, he was concerned only with immediate and controversial matters. This is not to say that he was a man of limited interests; his poems and essays ranged from the accession of a monarch to the stray dogs in the city, and it was this immediacy of interest which made his work popular among the common people.

Lizardi was imprisoned in 1812, since he was naïve enough to believe that the newly-declared freedom of the press in Mexico would permit him to attack the viceroy. He quickly learned his error, however, and it was only after eight months in jail that he managed to convince a new viceroy (by another, and more favorable, commentary) that he was just an incautious scribbler who could be safely released. Lizardi now realized that his outspoken attacks on the clergy and civil authorities could not be repeated, at least not in the same overt form, and the result was the first novel in Hispanic America.

Why were there no novels before 1815? Spain had produced many, there was ample subject matter in the New World, writers of ability and imagination were not lacking, but no novel was forthcoming. There must have been a most compelling reason, and it was obviously the Inquisition. The *Junta de Censura* had classified novels as *"materias profanas y fabulosas é historias fingidas,"* and there was no more to be said, at least so far as obedient Catholics were concerned.

The ban applied to both writing and importation of such fiction, but the law was enforceable only to a limited degree. Spell assures us that there was a certain amount of clandestine circulation of novels in Mexico before 1700, and by 1800 much foreign literature was available.[12] Lizardi was therefore familiar with the genre, certainly with picaresque novels in his own language, and it is not surprising that he turned novelist when he needed a new medium for presenting his ideas to the public.

The specific situation apparently developed in 1815, when he realized that the continuing suppression of his articles would not cease in the course of time. He had devoted some five years of his life to antagonizing the Government and the

Church, and now the authorities combined (or were they ever really separate in Mexico?) to silence his troublesome voice.

Lizardi determined to try his luck with a novel, hoping that the censors would be deceived by the apparently innocuous story, and mollified by the didactic frosting. Whether they actually didn't see the real meaning of the tale, as Brushwood alleges,[13] or perhaps were deceived by reading it in installments, as Spell believes,[14] the first three volumes were passed and printed within a six-month period. In the fourth volume Lizardi attacked the tradition of slavery, and this was the flag that caught the censor's eye. The remainder of the book was hurriedly prohibited and was, in fact, not printed until after the author's death in 1827.

It is logical to consider *El Periquillo Sarniento* as picaresque, but only careful analysis can determine the validity of the classification. The purpose for which it was written, the professional experience of the author, the limits imposed upon the genre and the omnipresent danger of retaliation must all be regarded at each step by the critic, as they were by Lizardi himself.

To begin with the positive side of the scale, there is no doubt that Lizardi was aware of the works which we regard as fundamentally picaresque: *Lazarillo de Tormes, Guzmán de Alfarache,* etc. He would logically have patterned his work upon them as the novels he knew. Periquillo certainly explores the less desirable areas of the world in which he is required to survive, moves from master to master, relates the story in the first person, past tense, and comes to a virtuous end. The incidents and stories are usually distasteful, frequently scatological, and it is social criticism which occupies the hero (or anti-hero) and the reader.

Nevertheless, at the risk of painting with too large a brush, and too free a hand, I suggest that none, or all, of these traditionally decisive criteria can stand against the single overwhelming argument to the contrary: Lizardi's reason for writing the book.

It is utterly incorrect to assume that Lizardi regarded *El Periquillo Sarniento* as a work of literary art, and an end in itself, as a modern professional novelist such as Proust or Mann might do. The genre was new to Lizardi as a writer, and I have shown that he turned to it only when his former vehicles, the pamphlet and periodical, were effectively forbidden to him by the government. In fact, although Lizardi produced four books altogether, he seems always to have regarded himself as a journalist, since he returned to his earlier direct pamphleteering in 1820, as soon as the Inquisition and the *Junta de Censura* were abolished.

Perhaps the most conclusive proof that *El Periquillo Sarniento* is not a picaresque novel is that Periquillo is not a pícaro! He is born of respectable middle-class parents, receives extensive education, and is accepted by the Church. Again and again he is rescued from hardship and poverty, and offered security, employment, and respectability, only to gamble away his money and throw away his opportunities. Could this poor, helpless fool be a personality based upon Guzmán or Lazarillo? Periquillo may, by a generous stretch of the term, be considered an anti-hero, but he is certainly no pícaro, and all the formal trappings of the book cannot make him into one.

Another vital critical point is that the biting, sarcastic tone of the generic Spanish picaresque tale is totally absent. Lizardi's satire is tempered with a most unpicaresque feeling of sympathy for the very people he is satirizing. His obvious desire, since he believes in the essential goodness of men, is to instruct them in order that they may undo the evil state unto which a corrupt society has brought them. This is in direct contrast to the Iberian picaresque novel, which satirizes and condemns social types and then leaves them with a curse instead of a blessing.

Quevedo was a pessimist—Lizardi was an optimist, and he wrote *El Periquillo Sarniento* in the firm belief that all he needed to do was to tell men how to live better lives, and they would do it gladly.

Lizardi's only other important book was *Don Catrín de la Fachenda,* which appeared in 1820. This was actually his fourth and last novel, and although it is of considerably less literary and social value than *El Periquillo Sarniento* it forms a most interesting companion piece. The two stories contrast in enough specific ways that Lizardi may have intended them to be regarded as a pair.

The protagonist, Don Catrín, begins with a disrespect for his family which is almost reminiscent of Guzmán, and this attitude continues for the remainder of his sordid life. Beginning with a respectable appointment as a military cadet, Catrín becomes in startling succession a pimp, gambler, convict, croupier, thug, robber, and finally beggar. He contracts venereal disease, dropsy, loses a wounded leg through amputation, and finally dies alone and deserted in a hospital room, almost to the exhausted and distressed reader's relief. It is not an inspiring tale...

A major point of contrast between the two works is that *El Periquillo Sarniento* has countless pages of sermonizing and virtuous exhortation (almost all of which have been carefully deleted by Katherine Anne Porter in her effort to improve upon the author),[15] and *Don Catrín de la Fachenda* is remarkably free of didacticism. There are no moral digressions, no lectures, no repentance, and the end is unedifying, to say the least. It is true that Cándido does provide a highly moral summation, but this is so patently Lizardi speaking through the flimsy *persona* that it is almost an epilogue, rather than a final scene, especially since it ends with an epitaph in the form of a sonnet.

Don Catrín goes downhill steadily, almost from the very start of the story; he ends utterly defeated, and there is not even slight justification for regarding the tale as a picaresque novel. In fact, one is tempted to say with Cándido, "!Ojalá no tenga imitadores!"

The comments above lead to an inevitable conclusion: if Lizardi worked in the vein of *picarismo,* he did so only in the hope that it would serve to slip his topical social commentary

past the suspicious eyes of the *Junta de Censura,* and he had
no particular concern with fidelity to the prototypes. Both *El
Periquillo Sarniento* and *Don Catrín de la Fachenda* exhibit
many of the characteristics of the Spanish picaresque novels,
the type with which Lizardi was familiar, but neither of his
principal characters is a pícaro. This situation is actually the
fundamental definition of *picarismo* in the Hispanic
American novel.

Following Lizardi, the works of longer fiction drift further
and further into *costumbrismo,* which considers the behavior
of the common people rather than the problems of a specific
individual. Lizardi himself was, of course, an early member of
this group of writers, but his intent was critical and crusading, rather than merely descriptive. With the passage of time
this emphasis changed, until it was almost entirely a matter
of description, with only enough comment to justify the
story, and to hold the reader's interest.

In the decades following Lizardi, one of the writers most
directly in his tradition was Don Manuel Payno, who was a
major contributor to the Mexican novel. He, too, was not a
professional novelist, but rather a journalist, who was in-
tensely aware of the era in which he lived, and who wrote
about everything which caught his interest. His most
important contribution to literature is his first novel, *El fistol
del diablo,* which appeared in 1845.

This was the first full-length novel to appear in Mexico
after Lizardi's work. Payno's book, although loosely organized and episodic, is more *costumbrismo* than *picarismo,*
however, since it is concerned primarily with the dress, behavior, and language of the common people. Social criticism
is not the purpose. The book cannot then be regarded as a
picaresque novel, but it is important to this study because it
is the link between Lizardi's transitional novel and what may
be regarded as genuine *telúrico*—the people in their home-
land, rather than merely as laboratory specimens in a bottle.

Unlike Lizardi, Payno was concerned with producing a

readable book—not a useful and moral lesson. He used almost any device which he believed would interest his readers, depending principally upon rapid and changing action, in which there is almost no time for author intervention to point up a moral. *El fistol del diablo* is almost structureless, partly, perhaps, because it was published *" de folletin"* or as a newspaper serial over a two-year period, but even more because Payno was concerned with his long series of incidents, rather than a tight plot. Aside from its position in the history of the genre, the work is more highly regarded for its historical records of folklore and the life of the people, than as a work of literature.

One might assume that picarismo was now ended in Mexico, except as a mild and occasional element, but there was one major reappearance of the tradition. In 1938 *La vida inútil de Pito Pérez* appeared, and there can be no doubt that the author, José Rubén Romero, intended to write a picaresque novel.

Although there is a clear autobiographical element in the book, the structural pattern which Romero selected places it within the scope of this study. He thought of himself as a pícaro, and a man mistreated by a hostile society. It was easy for him, and probably a satisfactory *katharsis,* to select the local ne'er-do-well as the hero of the tale, and describe his pilgrimage through life as a series of disreputable incidents of rather questionable taste.

Pito is a clear reference to Lazarillo and Guzmán in his declared belief that the foundations of social behavior are hypocrisy and selfishness. What may be a most useful comparison, and one which I have not seen suggested before, is that Pito Pérez is, in several ways, comparable to John Steinbeck's wonderful Cannery Row and Tortilla Flat Mexican-Americans. There is the precise negation of social values in Danny, Piton, and Big Joe that creates the "useless life" with which Romero is concerned. It would be interesting to know if Steinbeck and Romero knew each other's tales, or whether there is a common attitude to be found in Mexican and Mexican-American *paisanos,* without regard to the side of the Rio Grande on which they live.

Mexico, and all of the other Latin American countries, were now entering a period of great expansion and social development. Population increase, continued contact with other nations of the world, especially the United States, and the effects of World War II effectively ended the remaining tendency to medieval Spanish tradition. Instead of accepting humbly the amused tolerance of the rest of the world, Latin America began to assume a rightful position in the matter of international relationships, and to move forward toward new ideas in art and literature.

It is to be hoped that no Latin American will ever forget his Iberian literary heritage—but there is no more reason for picarismo in Mexico, Peru, or Argentina than in any other growing, modern nation. Until the cities of Latin America reach a point beyond their optimum, until there are extra human beings of no value to society, and until a social stratification which excludes mercy for Lazarillo develops anew, we cannot look for the pícaro in Mexico, Central, or South America again.

11

Modern Picarismo

In order to consider 20th century America as a possible background for the pícaro, it is first necessary to refresh one's acquaintance with the *Siglo de Oro,* since it will be shown that there was far more than an indebtedness—there was a direct resemblance.

La Novela Picaresca was founded upon the clear understanding that nothing in life was unsuitable to the author's pen. While the Inquisition not infrequently stepped in to declare a *non imprimatur,* the general reading public was not squeamish, and what was to be seen in the streets was quite acceptable upon the printed page.

The result was that gore, hardship, and tragedy are sprinkled liberally throughout the pages of *Lazarillo de Tormes, Guzmán de Alfarache, Celestina,* and the rest of the canon. It seems almost as if there were a continuing competition to portray the worst possible situations in the most vivid manner.

What else is 20th century American Naturalism?

As early as 1894, Henry Demarest Lloyd launched a vicious campaign against Standard Oil Co. with *Wealth Against Commonwealth. McClure's Magazine* sponsored Lincoln Steffens in a series of exposés which eventually comprised *The Shame of the Cities* (1904), and Ida M. Tarbell topped the list with her *History of the Standard Oil Company.*

The "muckrakers" were well underway in the non-fiction and magazine serial field, and it was inevitable that their attacks should begin to affect fiction as well. In Europe, for at least fifteen years, Emile Zola had been leading a group of writers bent upon introducing realism into the novel, and now the lightning struck in America as well.

Due partly, perhaps, to the depression of the 1890's, partly to the end of a Victorianism which was essentially unproductive and which could not, therefore, continue indefinitely, and partly to a natural reaction to imperfectly digested industrialization, America crossed the century divide, and discovered that, not a "bully" shining plateau, but rather a frightening gulf lay before it. Shaken and scared, Americans suddenly realized that a period of trouble was just ahead, and the writers of novels began the thankless process of showing their readers wherein the danger lay.

Frank Norris was one of these, perhaps the earliest, and although McTeague was not a pícaro, he must be mentioned here, not so much for what Norris said, but rather for the way he took of saying it. Carvel Collins credits Norris with importing European Naturalism into the literature of America, and this seems an accurate statement. Although there is realism aplenty in the works of Charles Brockden Brown, Hamlin Garland, Stephen Crane, and others who preceded Norris, the straightforward, unabashed description for the sole purpose of emphasizing human degradation seems to have appeared first in this country in Norris' novels.

His hero, McTeague, eats "thick gray soup; heavy underdone meat, very hot on a cold plate" and, when he wakes from the predator-like sleep following his gorging, "cropfull, stupid, and warm" he finishes the rest of his flat and stale beer, and then plays the six tunes he knows on the concertina. The author goes to some effort to point out that "these were [McTeague's] only pleasures—to eat, to smoke, to sleep, and to play upon his concertina."[1]

This air of animal functions and pleasures is the keynote of the book and, indeed, of most of Norris' work. Negation of the esthetic point of view, of the artistic or intellectual, is apparent in almost every one of his characters, and life in his books is like the thick, gray soup—totally lacking in the more delicate seasonings.

One of several reasons why McTeague is not a picaro is that his honest brutality is inadequate to deal with the Marcus Schoulers of this world; as a result, defeat, first social and eventually vital, is his inevitable end. This was one of the tenets of so much naturalistic literature to follow: we have left the Garden, but not the Serpent!

In the matter of technique, Frank Norris set another precedent. For the first time, an American novelist set out to acquire factual knowledge which he did not possess, for the purpose of adding effective realism to his story. Many writers of that period proved the value of specialized knowledge, especially Rudyard Kipling and Joseph Conrad, but now this author went to the Harvard library to learn the technical aspects of dentistry, thereby adding additional verisimilitude to an already convincing narrative. It is this relentless attention to detail which will prove to be one of the distinguishing characteristics of American prose fiction from the turn of the century to the present, just as it was in the *Siglo de Oro*. In fact, some American authors will depend almost entirely upon detail for effect.

Norris himself referred to Theodore Dreiser's *Sister Carrie* as the book which "pleased me as well as any novel I have read in *any* form, published or otherwise."[2] This is a most interesting opinion, since it not only endorsed a triumph of evil over good, but sponsored the reincarnation of Justina in America.

In its 20th century American form, the picaresque novel underwent certain alterations, the most immediately apparent being the raised physical standard at which the characters live. There was almost no poverty of the abject, starvation level to which the *Siglo de Oro* was accustomed. Instead, there was a minimum level which provided food, clothing, a roof, and not much more. Of far greater importance to Dreiser, and other naturalists, was the intellectual deprivation, which resulted in the life of a zoo animal for so many human beings: fed and protected, but totally without provision for improvement or freedom. Carrie Meeber's sister Minnie, and her brother-in-law Hanson[3] are intended to represent this frighteningly large group, and to the banality of their lives Dreiser attributes much of his Carrie's subsequent behavior. The two men in her life, Drouet, the "Goodtime Charlie" of the period, and Hurstwood, the weak, indecisive bigamist and thief who eventually degenerates completely and commits suicide, are presented neither as heroes nor as villains, but rather simply as types which are always attracted to the Carries of this world.

She uses first her relatives, then each of the two men in turn, and finally her own ability in show business to reach an undreamed-of success, unmarred by any pangs of conscience. Like Justina, she has used her body to achieve security, and not all the Mrs. Frank Doubledays in America can change this particular amoral pragmatism by forbidding publication of a book. On the contrary, perhaps for the first time, the seamy side of life, which was accepted in Europe so many years earlier as suitable for literary discussion, was being portrayed in American to warn us that the Garden was now far, far behind.

Dreiser produced another novel of this type in 1925, when he wrote *An American Tragedy,* but a new note of defeatism had entered his thinking. Caring little for the consequences, Carrie Meeber won her battle with life because she was stronger and more relentless than anyone she encountered— Clyde Griffiths loses his because he is simply too weak. His sensitivity, his insecurity, and the shame he has always felt for his parents' evangelical activities have combined to leave him the victim of every emotional crosswind which blows across his path.

Clyde flees from his home because of involvement in a hit-and-run accident which is not his fault, he seduces (or is seduced by) Roberta Alden, and then murders her in order to conceal her pregnancy and leave himself free for the socially desirable Sondra Finchley. Clyde's humiliating end in the electric chair is the culmination of an ineffectual effort to live, and it is symbolic that even his death is determined and effected by other men.

This is clearly a direct antithesis of the pícaro, since the circumstances are entirely characteristic, but the personality of the protagonist is opposite to that of Lazarillo. The society in which this action takes place is indeed hostile, the resources of the youth are (albeit sometimes voluntarily) his own wits and little else, and his survival could have resulted only from superior perception and amoral behavior. Nevertheless, there is a lack of that personal vitality which is absolutely necessary in the fact of superior odds, if the desires of the individual are to be forced upon the entire society. Because he is never in control of his own destiny, and eventually loses his battle, Clyde is never a pícaro.

The same is true of a succession of American anti-heroes, such as F. Scott Fitzgerald's Jay Gatsby, James Farrell's Studs Lonigan, and J.D. Salinger's Holden Caulfield, each of whom wishes that he could stand up to life, but none of whom has the essential vitality which made Lazarillo's winning possible.

Nevertheless, in spite of a distinct lack of specifically picaresque personalities in modern American literature, there is a major indebtedness to the *Siglo de Oro:* the return from moral romanticism to the sordid verbal scenery and endless detail which are fundamental characteristics of the picaresque novel.

Such matters as smells, putrid food, disease, and bodily pain were normal subjects for Fernando de Rojas and Juan Ruiz, and they again became acceptable, after a Victorian hiatus, in the works of such authors as James Farrell and

John Steinbeck. The cycle—realism to prudery to realism—
was completed in the early years of the present century, and
it was a picaresque naturalism that it returned to the novel.

The emphasis on, and acceptance of, lurid sex scenes in
modern American fiction seems a logical, almost inevitable,
extension of this realism. Although evolving sex mores are
hardly to be explained adequately by this, or any other
simple reason, it is plausible to assume that a rapidly de-
creasing reticence in physical matters, and a rapidly
increasing tolerance of anything the author cares to write,
must be based upon a specific springboard, and that the modern "sex novel" indicates no more than a willingness to go
further in this direction than literature has gone in the past.

The *Libro de Buen Amor,* while it is much more too, is
definitely pornographic in the modern legal sense, and there
is much in *Celestina* which could never pass the Hays office.
It is, therefore, only in the specific language of sexual functions that American novelists have exceeded the picaresque
writers, and it is precisely in portraying sexual activities for
the sake of sensation, not characterization, that they have
lost the humanistic aspects of *picarismo.*

Lazarillo and Justina did not lead happy lives, but even
without the happy (to them) endings, the reader is always
made to understand that they regarded life as essentially
good and worth living, regardless of how hard it might be.
Perhaps it is the loss of this basic belief in the value of life
itself which has resulted in the disappearance of the hero in
America outside of comic strips and Western movies.

Although this discussion concerned primarily with the
pícaro in 20th century America, not Europe, there is one
instance of European indebtedness which is so direct and
unmistakable that not to mention it would be inexcusable.

The most successful modern effort at creating a picaresque
personality in literature, although one cannot be certain that
it was intentional, is the extant fragmentary novel of Thomas
Mann, *Die Behenntnisse des Hochstaplers Felix Krull,* which
was begun in 1911.

It is fascinating to identify the many specific similarities between this work and *Lazarillo de Tormes,* beginning quite literally with birth. Both Felix and Lazarillo were born in close association with moving water, symbolizing their lack of social stability, the one in a feed mill on the river Tormes, and the other along the Rhine.

The fathers of both youths were notoriously dishonest, one with his "wounded" grain sacks and the other with a fraudulent wine business; although we have no grounds for believing Frau Krull quite the unabashed trollop that Señora Tormes unquestionably was, she was certainly not the excessively moral *hausfrau* either.

Lazarillo's mentor was the blind beggar, who taught him his first repertoire of tricks and devices for survival in a hostile world; Felix is indebted to the self-created "Professor" Schimmelpreester for similar favors. It is worth noting that these two disreputable Chirons are both entirely without shame or scruples, and share a cheerful acceptance of the fact that this is a cheating world, and the only problem to be considered is how to cheat best.

Less directly picaresque, but nevertheless not without distinct points of identification, is Mann's *Joseph und seine Brüder.* A little like John Erskine's treatment of Galahad,[4] the author regards the Biblical youth in a purely materialistic analysis as doing an excellent job of taking care of himself in the hostile Egyptian world by calmly deciding that the end of his survival, and the protection of his people, justifies whatever means he can most successfully employ, and the loss of a few Egyptians now and again need bother no one.

Instead of either a beggar of Spain or the good German "Professor" as mentor, Joseph is provided with Eliezer, the "oldest servant," and it is by no means insignificant that his patron diety, Hermes, is god of not only wayfarers but thieves as well.

Both of these works are labeled by Mann himself as *"Schelmenroman,"*[5] which is most readily and accurately translated as "picaresque novels." There are, to be sure, additional connotations to the German word, but none which contradict or invalidate the Spanish.

Nothing could better emphasize the intrinsic nature of the pícaro in western literatures than the fact that, apparently without consciously willing it, Thomas Mann in at least two novels gave birth to characters so directly identifiable with Lazarillo.

12

The Pícaro
as Anachronism

At the beginning of this discussion, a clear dividing line between *picarismo* and criminality was defined,[1] to which the writer has adhered carefully in defining literary personalities as falling within or without the group headed by Lazarillo de Tormes. The fundamental criterion has been, without exception, whether the youth was involved in his asocial and usually illegal activities as a last resort in a fight for simple physical survival in a hostile environment. If not, he must be regarded as a professional criminal who has chosen this means of gaining a living, instead of a socially acceptable pursuit which was equally available to him.

This definition is a satisfactory heuristic approach to the literatures of older societies and continues to be adequate in any normally organized society—normal, that is, in the degree to which the minutiae of human conduct are regulated. This comparatively extensive freedom no longer exists in America, however, and the criterion is therefore no longer valid.

Although at first glance this appears to be a rather sweeping statement, it can be substantiated both in the literature of the 20th century, and from our personal experience. Since the pícaro is usually considered to be a youth, it may be most effective to compare the famous escapades of the archetype, Lazarillo, to the conditions of a hypothetical boy in approximately similar circumstances in America today.

Allowing for the possibility of a broken home and his mother's subsequent miscegenation, the first impossibility is that a small boy should be apprenticed to a street beggar. He would be required to attend school, would be placed in a foster home or institution if necessary, and there is no legal street begging in America anyway. So one must begin by recognizing the impossibility in this country of Lazarillo's basic situation.

The Spanish boy, after disposing of the blind beggar to his own (and the reader's) satisfaction, then sets about finding his own next master and accepts service with a priest. This would be impossible in today's America, because he would be regarded as homeless and turned over to the suitable authorities for care and feeding, especially if he were to contact the Church. In fact, the fundamental motive of almost all of the pícaro's activities, hunger, is one which is quite literally non--existent in normal American life. Such organizations as the Salvation Army make provision for the feeding of hungry vagrants, and the State has full authority for the apprehension and institutionalization of homeless youths.

There is an entirely separate and, perhaps, even more apparent aspect of *picarismo* which cannot now exist in America without prompt government attention: juvenile delinquency. In many countries, especially those in which people are accustomed to hand-to-mouth survival, such as China and Mexico, theft is still common enough so that street venders and farmers must expect to be subjected to the depredations of the homeless. In America, however, with the exception of the melon patch and the apple orchard, theft of food is not regarded with social tolerance in any but the most desperate circumstances, such as John Steinbeck describes so vividly in *The Grapes of Wrath.*

The very fact that he makes such a point of hunger shows that the reader could be expected to react with shock and disbelief, rather than with the blasé acceptance of a 16th century reader in Spain. The youth who steals food in

America today is almost always labeled a juvenile delinquent, since the law assumes that it is not necessary to his physical survival. The State therefore sets about catching and caring for him, not for a punitive purpose, but in order to reeducate and train him as a useful member of society. In other words, to behave in a picaresque manner, a boy must today fight and run from those who are trying to feed, clothe, and educate him. It requires a distorted point of view, indeed, to believe that Lazarillo would run from a full belly and a warm place to sleep, when the only price to pay was to learn how to have them for the rest of his life!

The criterion to which this discussion refers is, therefore, altered from *picarismo* vs. crime, to juvenile delinquency vs. adult crime, which is quite a different dichotomy. In the first, there was a clear acceptability of one, and only by crossing the dividing line did the individual render himself unacceptable to society at large. In the second, he is equally unacceptable in either class, and it is only the specific authority and treatment which varies. In neither juvenile delinquency nor adult crime is there room for the social tolerance upon which the continued existence of a pícaro must depend.

A consciousness of this alteration is quite apparent in the works of such authors as James Farrell and Saul Bellow, who recognize that the need of the individual is now to survive morally and intellectually—not merely physically. Mark Twain recognized this trend in *The Adventures of Huckleberry Finn,* anticipating the current struggle to escape the bonds of an over-solicitous society. The difference is that now there is no Mississippi river on which one can float to freedom and self-realization. The pathway must now be sought within the individual's own being, because there is nowhere else to look for it.

No thinking American can be unaware of the tremendously complicated bureaucracy under which he lives, a governmental machine which is so huge that it is literally true that no man can fully grasp its ramifications. The moral desirability of such a father-machine, or its eventual effects upon the creators, is not germane to this discussion—the simple fact is that such a government *does* exist, and it affects every citizen in every aspect of his life.

This paternalism extends with particular direction to those individuals who are considered in need of physical care, and who have occasion to draw the attention of society to themselves. Once identified as a target for charity, such a person becomes the object of a relentless official campaign designed to result in his personal benefit, and the salving of the public conscience. As the population grows, so does the machine, and the very operation of the government has the effect of increasing the number of lives which might otherwise not require its care. Against such an overwhelming avalanche of good will, where can the pícaro go to be hungry?

Consideration has already been given to the effect upon *picarismo* of surplus population,[2] and one may not ignore the present population "explosion" in America. This country is still closer to the Frontier than to the *Siglo de Oro* in this regard, however, and the current increase in population cannot be regarded as a possible basis for the existence of future pícaros—at least not for many generations to come. Even automation is apparently having the effect of creating additional employment and prosperity. Surplus population, in the sense of human beings to be thrown away as useless, is not yet an admissible concept in America.

Where, then, in America, is there room for the pícaro?

The answer, unfortunately for the sake of literature to come, is that there is no room and may never again be. The conditions which produced Lazarillo were not unique, but they were of an era which the world will never see again. A mighty nation, once almost the greatest in the world, had fallen into decay, and there was no country willing or able to take it over. As a result, the chronic, low-grade social infection simply continued, generation after starving generation.

Other countries, more prosperous, felt the essential truth

in the literature which Spain produced, and realized that this boy was the same social misfit that had inspired Greek and Roman writers. Without the hindrance of copyright laws, they did not hesitate to adopt the type of tale which Quevedo, de Rojas, and Cervantes used so well. Although France, Germany, and Holland did not suffer from the same utter poverty and despair which was so characteristic of both Spain and her literature, they were nevertheless able to appreciate it. Since their problems, if not identical to Castile's, were not unrelated, they added the picaro to their literature and proved once again that this personality knew no national bounds but was common to all human society.

England, with the ready wit and devilish sense of humor so characteristic of the common man, took the picaro to its heart, and when *Lazarillo de Tormes* appeared in translation about 1568, it was hailed as the epitome of all rogue tales. Thomas Nashe produced *The Unfortunate Traveller* in 1594, and the era of the English novel had begun. For the next three centuries this form of literature would be the chosen genre of countless authors, many of whom would regard the essentially genuine personality of the picaro as their ideal protagonist. From Jack Wilton to Kim, the manly English youth who beat the heartless world at its own game would be remembered with pride and indulgence as a national hero.

The picaro must have stowed away on one of the boats crossing the Atlantic in the 17th century (who could picture Lazarillo buying a ticket?) and if his next costume was buckskins instead of rags, he was still the same resourceful devil-may-care boy who outwitted beggars and landed on his ragged feet wherever he happened to fall.

Always looking at the underside of life, never willing to accept people or institutions at any valuation but his own, he appeared first in colonial Pennsylvania, and later on a Mississippi raft. It was as well that he became conscious of the need to escape, since this raft trip was almost his last light-hearted adventure. America was starting to grow up, and there was less and less place for a boy who wanted to spend his life in living—not grow rich and respectable at the cost of independence.

Lazarillo had always had the knack of showing up the hardships and hypocrisies of life, but this had been incidental. He was really the hero of a good adventure story, and now the only place for him seemed to be in a sermon or on the lecture platform, as a horrible example. This provided few things to laugh about, and all that finally remained was the bitter reality which had been made platable for so many generations only by a hearty laugh.

Everywhere Lazarillo turned, there were people who knew better than he how he should behave. They fed him, dressed him, sent him to school—and nobody could tell him the reason for it all. It was just there to be done, and so they did it.

There is no room for Lazarillo in America anymore...

Nevertheless, Lazarillo is a basic part of humanity, and when he is expelled from one society he has no hesitation in changing his coat and his tongue. The pícaro is not national, not even international, but rather universal and eternal as long as there are men living together in groups.

Aristophanes is gone, and so is the gentle Cervantes; Nashe and Fielding with their biting satires will not come again, any more than will Kipling or Mark Twain. But before each of these, there were other authors, and none of them wrote the last picaresque novel, or found the last pícaro in his own country. So long as there is a Gogol to tell about the wonderful machinations of Chichikov in *Dead Souls,* or a Stendhal to follow the career of Julian Sorel in *Le Rouge et le Noir,* the pícaro will continue to occupy a very special place in literature.

Although this study has dealt almost exclusively with the English and American picaresque personality in the literature of recent centuries, it must be recognized that the same trend is entirely perceptible in other countries. Only the limitations of space and time have caused the specificity, which must not be interpreted as indicating a principal line of descent from the *Siglo de Oro.* The pícaro is to be found in the stories of almost every land, from the Greek and Turkish "Karagöz" theatre, to Boer tales of the veldt.

It is entirely possible that the unsuitability of the American scene for the continuation of the picaresque personality in literature will not extend to other countries— especially those at an earlier stage of social development. If so, their literature will continue to reflect the same type, and future generations of authors and readers will share the endless delights of the pícaro.

Notes

Chapter 1

1.   Frank Wadleigh Chandler, *The Literature of Roguery* (New York: Burt Franklin, 1958), p. 4.
2.   John Cleland, *Memoirs of a Woman of Pleasure.*
3.   Daniel Defoe, *The Fortunes and Misfortunes of the Famous Moll Flanders.*
4.   William Makepeace Thackeray, *Vanity Fair, A Novel Without a Hero.*

Chapter 2

1.   *La Traji-Comedia de Calisto y Melibea.*
2.   Juan Ruiz, *The Book of Good Loves,* trans. by Elisha K. Kane (New York: William Edwin Rudge, 1933).
3.   Fernando de Rojas, *La Celestina,* trans. by Lesley Byrd Simpson (Berkeley: University of California Press, 1955).
4.   Miduel de Cervantes Saavedra, *El Ingenioso Hidalgo Don Quixote de la Mancha—Primera Parte.*
5.   Antonio Enriquez Gomez, *El Siglo Pitagórico* (1644).
6.   Chandler, p. 5.
7.   Francisco de Quevedo y Villegas, *Historia de la Vida del Buscón llamado Don Pablos* (1626).
8.   Chander, p. 4.

Chapter 3

1.   Robert Alter, *Rogue's Progress* (Cambridge: Harvard University Press, 1964), pp. 2-10.

2.   Gerald Brennan, *The Literature of the Spanish People* (Cambridge: University Press, 1962), p. 99.

3.   *La vida de Tormes y de sus fortunas y adversidades* (1554), ch. II.

4.   René Wellek and Austin Warren, *Theory of Literature* (New York: Random House, 1949), p. 44.

5.   Ernest Mérimée, *A History of Spanish Literature*, trans. by S. Griswold Morley (New York: Holt, 1930), p. 203.

6.   Alter, *Rogue's Progress*, p. 39.

7.   Mariano Velázquez de la Cadena, *A New Pronouncing Dictionary of the Spanish and English Languages* (Chicago: Wilcox & Follett Co., 1955), p. 497.

8.   *Webster's New Twentieth Century Dictionary of the English Language, 2nd Edition* (Cleveland: World Publishing Co., 1962), p. 1355.

9.   Gary MacEóin, *Cervantes* (Milwaukee: Bruce Publ. Co., 1950), p. 65.

10.   Werner P. Friedrich, *Outline of Comparative Literature* (Chapel Hill: University of North Carolina Press, 1954), p. 111.

Chapter 4

1.   *Teatro del Hombre.*

Chapter 5

1.   This refers to the first installment. It was retranslated by Jean Chapelain in 1619, and reprinted eight times.

2.   The "conclusion" was added by de la Brentonne, and is not authorized by the original Spanish version.

3.   *Les Avantures de Monsieur d'Assoucy.*

Chapter 6

1.   I refer to the thirteenth century *Schwänke,* perhaps best represented by *Tül Eulenspiegel*, Pfaffer von Kalenberg, and Peter Lau.

Chapter 7

1.   John L. Heller and Raymond Leonard Grismer, "Seneca in the Celestinesque Novel," *Hispanic Review,* XII, 29.

2.   Ernest A. Baker, *The History of the English Novel* (London: H.F. & G. Witherby Ltd., 1937), IV, 17.

3.   Apuleius, *The Golden Ass,* ed. by Charles Whibley, trans. by William Adlington (London: David Nutt, 1893), Intro. x.

4.   Donald B. Sands, *The History of Reynard the Fox* (Cambridge, Mass.: Harvard University Press, 1960), p. 3.

5.   George K. Anderson, *Old and Middle English Literature* (New York: Crowell-Collier, 1962), p. 142.

6.   Sands, p. 3.

7.   Charles Swan (trans.), *Gesta Romanorum* (London: George Routledge & Sons, 1905), preface xii.

8.   (v. pp. 6-7.)

Chapter 8

1.   (v. p. 20.)

2.   Hardin Craig, *The Literature of the English Renaissance* (New York: Collier, 1962), p. 139.

3.   *Lazarillo*, p. 33.

4.   Chandler, p. 235.

5.   Martin S. Day, *The History of English Literature to 1660* (Garden City: Doubleday & Co., 1963), p. 232.

6.   Edward Arber, ed., *A Transcript of the Registers of the Company of Stationers of London, 1554-1640* (London: 1875), p. 173.

7.   Thomas Nashe, *The Unfortunate Traveller,* ed. by H.F.B. Brett-Smith (Boston: Houghton, Mifflin, 1920), pp. 95-96.

8.   Baker, p. 45.

9.   Chandler, p. 193.

10.   J.J. Jusserand, *The English Novel in the Time of Shakespeare,* trans. by Elizabeth Lee (London: T. Fisher Unwin, 1901), p. 294.

11.   Ibid., p. 308.

12.   Henry Fielding, *The History of Tom Jones.*

13.   *The Welch Traveller, or the Unfortunate Welchman* (1657).

14.   Chandler, p. 212, n. 1.

15.   *Beso los manos* ("I kiss your hands").

16.   Richard Head, *The English Rogue* (London: Henry Marsh, 1665), I, xiii.

17.   Ibid., p. iii.

18.   Wilbur L. Cross, *Development of the English Novel* (New Haven: Yale University Press, 1900), pp. 19-20.

19.   Head, pp. 47-53.

20.   Chandler, p. 286.

21.   Cross, p. 204.
22.   Chandler, p. 328.
23.   Day, p. 223.
24.   Velázquez, p. 497.
25.   Webster, p. 1355.
26.   Walter Raleigh, *The English Novel* (New York: Charles Scribner's Sons, 1911), p. 135.
27.   Chandler, p. 292.
28.   Robert Alter, perhaps unthinkingly, refers to Moll as an "anti-heroine," which is quite unjustifiable. The fundamental characteristic of an anti-hero is that he ultimately loses his battle against life and society, and Moll, like the *pícara* she is, ends her career secure and respectable.
29.   *An Apology for the Life of Mrs. Shamela Andrews* (1741).
30.   *The History of the Adventures of Joseph Andrews and of his friend Mr. Abraham Adams, Written in imitation of the manner of Cervantes, author of Don Quixote.*
31.   Henry Fielding, *The Life of Jonathan Wild the Great* (London: T. Curson Hansard, 1806), "A List of the Principal Characters."
32.   (v. p. 18.)
33.   *Lazarillo*, p. 53.
34.   Aurelien Digeon, *The Novels of Fielding* (London: George Routledge & Sons, 1925), p. 93.
35.   Chandler, p. 308.
36.   Ibid., p. 64.
37.   Tobias Smollett, *Ferdinand, Count Fathom.*
38.   Ibid.
39.   Tobias Smollett, *Roderick Random.*
40.   Smollett, *Ferdinand, Count Fathom*, p. 372.
41.   Baker, p. 216.
42.   Ibid.
43.   (v. p. 3.)
44.   No. 249.
45.   No. 343.
46.   Raleigh, p. 191.
47.   Cleland, *Memoirs*, p. v.
48.   (v. n. 28, above.)
49.   *Pamela's Conduct in High Life.*
50.   (v. Hogarth's "Harlot's Progress," 1737).
51.   Cleland, *Memoirs*, p. 198.
52.   William Forsyth, *The Novels and Novelists of the Eighteenth Century* (London: John Murray, 1871), p. 152.
53.   Day, p. 503.

54.   William Browne Hockley (?), *Pandurang Hàrì or Memoirs of a Hindoo* (London: Henry S. King & Co., 1873), p. 26.

55.   Robert Morss Lovett and Helen Sard Hughes, *The History of the Novel in England* (Cambridge, Mass.: Houghton, Mifflin, 1932), p. 204.

56.   Ibid., p. 208.

57.   Chandler, pp. 362-363.

58.   William Harrison Ainsworth, *Jack Sheppard* (London: George Routledge & Sons, 1895), p. 54.

59.   Ibid., p. 285.

60.   (v. p. 23.)

61.   Charles Dickens, *The Posthumous Papers of the Pickwick Club.*

62.   (v. p. 54.)

63.   Chandler, p. 462.

64.   Thackeray, *Vanity Fair,* p. 7.

65.   Ibid., p. 576.

66.   Ibid., p. 720.

Chapter 9

1.   Nelson Manfred Blake, *A History of American Life and Thought* (New York: McGraw-Hill, 1963), p. 315.

2.   Miguel de Cervantes Saavedra, *Novelas Ejemplares* trans. by Samuel Putnam (New York: Viking Press, 1950).

3.   (v. p. 2.)

4.   Wilbur Fisk Gordy, *History of the United States* (New York: Charles Scribner's Sons, 1922), p. 385.

5.   Ibid., p. 187.

6.   Julian W. Abernathy, *American Literature* (New York: Maynary, Merrill, & Co., 1902), p. 102.

7.   Darrel Abel, *American Literature* (New York: Barron, 1963), I, 302.

8.   Charles Brockden Brown, *Arthur Mervyn or Memoirs of The Year 1793* (New York: Holt, Rinehart and Winston, 1962), p. 316.

9.   Fred Lewis Pattee, *The First Century of American Literature* (New York: D. Appleton-Century, 1935), pp. 156-157.

10.   Abernathy, p. 96.

11.   William B. Cairns, *A History of American Literature* (New York: Oxford University Press, 1930), p. 147.

12.   Pattee, p. 157.

13.   Ludwig Lewisohn, *The Story of American Literature* (New York: Random House, 1932), p. 54.

14.　　Abel, p. 278.
15.　　Hugh Henry Brackenridge, *Modern Chivalry* (New York: American Book Co., 1937), p. 44.
16.　　(v. p. 61.)
17.　　Ludwig Bemelmans, *The Eye of God* (New York: Viking Press, 1949, p. 191).
18.　　Sculley Bradley, *et al*, eds., *The American Tradition in Literature* (New York: W.W. Norton, 1962), II, 260, n. 1.
19.　　Leslie A. Fiedler, *Love and Death in the American Novel* (Cleveland: World Publishing Co., 1960), p. 575.
20.　　William Dean Howells, *My Literary Passions* (New York: Harper & Brothers, 1895), pp. 38-39.
21.　　Henry Wadsworth Longfellow, "The Spanish Student" in *The Complete Poetical Works of Henry Wadsworth Longfellow* (Boston: Houghton Mifflin, 1902), p. 31.
22.　　Howells, p. 143.
23.　　William Dean Howells, *The Rise of Silas Lapham* (New York: Random House, 1951), p. 4.

Chapter 10

1.　　Margarita Blondet Hogan, "Picaresque Literature in Spanish America," (unpublished dissertation, Columbia University, 1953), p. 36.
2.　　José J. Real Díaz, "Don Alonso Carrió de la Vandera, autor del 'Lazarillo de ciegos caminantes,' " *Biblioteca de Autores Españoles* (Madrid: 1959), CXII, 245-277.
3.　　Alonso Carrió de la Vandera, *El Lazarillo de Ciegos caminantes*, trans. by Walter C. Kline (Bloomington: University of Indiana Press, 1967), p. 299.
4.　　*Ibid.*, chapter 22.
5.　　Enrique Anderson-Imbert, *Spanish-American Literature*, trans. by John Va. Falconieri, 2nd edition revised by Elaine Malley (Detroit: Wayne State University Press, 1969), p. 167.
6.　　Fernando Alegría, *Breve Historia de la novela hispano-americana* (Mexico: Ediciones de Andrea, 1959), p. 13.
7.　　Hogan, p. 94.
8.　　Jacques-Charles Brunet, *Manuel de Libraire et de l'Amateur de Livres* (Paris: Librairie de Firmin Didot Frères, Fils et Cie., 1965), p. 950.
9.　　Frank Wadleigh Chandler, *Romances of Roguery* (New York: Burt Franklin, 1961), p. 199.
10.　　Velásquez, p. 406.

11.   Alegría, p. 9.

12.   J.R. Spell, "The Genesis of the First Mexican Novel," *Hispania,* XIV (1931), 53-58.

13.   John S. Brushwood, *Mexico in its Novel* (Austin: University of Texas Press, 1966), p. 65.

14.   Spell, *op. cit.*.

15.   José Joaquín Fernández de Lizardi, *El Periquillo Sarniento,* trans. by Eugene Pressly, intro. by Katherine Anne Porter (Garden City: Doubleday, Doran, 1942).

Chapter 11

1.   Frank Norris, *McTeague* (New York: Holt, Rinehart and Winston, 1962), p. 1.

2.   Robert H. Elias, *Theodore Dreiser: Apostle of Nature* (New York: Alfred A. Knopf, 1949), p. 111.

3.   Theodore Dreiser, *Sister Carrie* (New York: Random House, 1932), p. 14.

4.   John Erskine, *Galahad, Enough of his Life to Explain his Reputation* (Indianapolis: Bobbs-Merrill, 1926).

5.   Karl Kerenyi, *Romandichtung and Mythologie* (Zurich: 1945), p. 83.

Chapter 12

1.   (v. p. 3.)

2.   (v. p. 73.)

Chronological List of Works

Although this study divides works according to basic national groupings, the fundamental organization must, of necessity, be chronological.

It is therefore of the utmost importance that the reader remain aware of the parallel development of picaresque literature in different cultures. Failure to do so will inevitably result in the illusion of simple indebtedness, and a disregard of the simultaneous creation of related but quite original stories. As a further aid, the chronology will suggest works which might have been known to any author, by providing dates of important translations.

The following list of books discussed in this study should be consulted at each significant stage, since by doing this the reader will be reminded of the several national contributions to the genre in any given period.

1661   *La Fouyne de Seville*
1662   *Avantures Tragicomiques du Chevalier de la Gaillardise*
-------   German sequel to *Guzmán de Alfarache*
1663   *The English Rogue*
1668   *Periquillo, él de las Gallineras*
1669   *Der Abentheurliche Simplicissimus*
1670   *Trutz Simplex*
1683   *Ungarischer oder Dacianischer Simplicissimus*
1695   *De Vermakelyke Avanturier*
1700   *Mémoires de M. d'Artagnan*
1703   *Mémoires du Chevalier Hassard*
1707   *De Geleerde Advokaat of de Bespotte Drüivedief*
-------   *The Spanish Libertines*
-------   *The Country Jilt*
1708   *L'infortuné Napolitain ou Les Avantures du Seigneur Rozelli*
1710   *Les Libertines en Campagne*
-------   *Tatler* No. 249 (Steele)
1712   *Spectator* No. 343 (Addison)
1713   *Mémoires du Chevalier du Compte de Gramont*
-------   *Les Tours de Mâitre Gonin*
1715   *Gil Blas*
1719   *The Life and Strange Surprising Adventures of Robinson Crusoe*
1722   *The Fortunes and Misfortunes of the Famous Moll Flanders*
-------   *The History and Remarkable Life of Colonel Jacques*
1724   *Roxanna, or the Fortunate Mistress*
1732   *Avantures de M. Robert Chevalier, dit de Beauchêne*
1734   *Histoire d'Estevanille Gonzalés*
1736   *Bachelier de Salamanque*
1740   *Pamela; or Virtue Rewarded*
1741   *An Apology for the Life of Mrs. Shamela Andrews*
1742   *The History of the Adventures of Joseph Andrews*
1743   *Simplicissimus Redivivus*
-------   *Journey from this World to the Next*
-------   *The History of the Life of the Late Jonathan Wild the Great*
1748   *The Adventures of Rodrick Random*
1749   English translation of *Gil Blas* (Smollett)
-------   *The History of Tom Jones, a Foundling*
1751   *The History of Pompey the Little*
1752   *Female Quixote*
1753   *The Adventures of Ferdinand Count Fathom*
1755   English translation of *Don Quixotte* (Smollett)
1760   *Polly Honeycomb*

1900	*Sister Carrie*
1901	*Kim*
1904	*The Shame of the Cities*
1911	*Die Behenntnisse des Hochstaplers Felix Krull*
1925	*An American Tragedy*
1933	*Joseph und seine Brüder*
1939	*The Grapes of Wrath*

Bibliography

The following selected bibliography is intended to serve the reader in two ways:

Every work cited in or considered essential to this book is listed, in order to provide an alphabetical guide by author. This is particularly important in a scholarly field noted for duplication of titles.

Although it is unreasonable to attempt a comprehensive list of every work consulted or read in this study, certain authors are responsible for a contribution of such importance that failure to mention them is unthinkable. Their works, including certain English translations of especial value, are accordingly included.

Abel, Darrel. *American Literature.* 3 vols. Great Neck, N.Y.: Barron's, 1963.

Abernethy, Julian W. *American Literature.* New York: Maynard, Merrill, 1902.

Ainsworth, W[illiam] Harrison. *Jack Sheppard.* London: George Routledge & Sons, 1895.

Aldridge, John W. *After the Lost Generation.* New York: Farrar, Straus, 1963.

Alegría, Fernando. *Breve Historia de la novela hispano-americana.* Mexico: Ediciones de Andrea, 1959.

Alter, Robert. *Rogue's Progress: Studies in the Picaresque Novel.* Cambridge: Harvard University Press, 1964.

Anderson, George K., ed. *Old and Middle English Literature.* New York: Crowell-Collier, 1962.

Anderson-Imbert, Enrique. *Spanish-American Literature.* Trans. by John V. Falconieri, 2nd edition revised by Elaine Malley. Detroit: Wayne State University Press, 1969.

Apuleius. *The Golden Ass.* Trans. by William Adlington. London: H.F. & G. Witherby, 1937.

Baker, Ernest A. *The History of the English Novel.* 10 vols. London: David Nutt, 1937.

Bemelmans, Ludwig. *The Eye of God.* New York: Viking Press, 1949.

Blake, Nelson Manfred. *A History of American Life and Thought.* New York: McGraw Hill, 1963.

Bleiberg, Germán *et al,* eds. *Dictionario de Literatura Española* (segunda edicion). Madrid: Revista de Occidente, 1953.

Brenan, Gerald. *The Literature of the Spanish People.* Cambridge: University Press, 1962.

Brackenridge, Hugh Henry. *Modern Chivalry.* New York: American Book Co., 1937.

Bradley, Sculley, Richard Croom Beatty and E. Hudson Long. *The American Tradition in Literature.* 2 vols. New York: W.W. Norton Co., 1962.

Brady, Agnes Marie and Laurel Herbert Turk, eds. *Classical Spanish Readings.* New York: D. Appleton-Century, 1933.

Brunet, Jacques-Charles. *Manuel du Libraire et de L'Amateur de Livres.* Paris: Librairie de Firmin Didot Frères, Fils et Cie., 1865.

Brushwood, John S. *Mexico in its Novel: A Nation's Search for Identity.* Austin: University of Texas Press, 1966.

Bourland, Caroline B. "Boccaccio and the 'Decameron' in Castilian and Catalán Literature," *Revue Hispanique,* XII, 1905, 12-32.

-----. *The Short Story in Spain in the Seventeenth Century.* Northampton, Mass.: Smith College Press, 1927.

Cadena, Mariano Velásquez de la. *A New Pronouncing Dictionary of the Spanish and English Languages.* Chicago: Wilcox & Follett, 1955.

Cairns, William B. *A History of American Literature.* New York: Oxford University Press, 1930.

Calderón, Ventura García. "La Literatura Peruana." *Revue Hispanique,* XXXI (1914), 305-391.

Cameron, Wallace J. "The Theme of Hunger in the Spanish Picaresque Novel." Unpublished dissertation, State University of Iowa, 1956. (Microfilm).

Carrió de la Vandera, Alonso. *El Lazarillo de Ciegos caminantes.* Ed. by José Luis Busaniche. Buenos Aires: Ediciones Argentinas Solar, 1942.

----. *El Lazarillo: A Guide for Inexperienced Travelers Between Buenos Aires and Lima.* Trans. by Walter C. Kline. Bloomington: University of Indiana Press, 1967.

Cela, Camilo José. *Nuevas andanzas y desaventuras de Lazarillo de Tormes.* Barcelona: Editorial Noguer, 1963.

Chandler, Frank Wadleigh. *The Literature of Roguery*. 2 vols. New York: Burt Franklin, 1958.

-----. *Romances of Roguery*. New York: Burt Franklin, 1961.

Chandler, Richard E. and Kessel Schwartz. *A New History of Spanish Literature*. Baton Rouge: Louisiana State University Press, 1961.

Chase, Richard. *The American Novel and its Tradition*. Garden City: Doubleday, 1957.

Cleland, John. *Memoirs of a Woman of Pleasure*. New York: G.P. Putnam's Sons, 1963.

Coester, Alfred. *The Literary History of Spanish America*. New York: Macmillan, 1928.

Cohen, J.M. *Latin American Writing Today*. Baltimore: Penguin Books, 1967.

Craig, Hardin. *The Literature of the English Renaissance*. New York: Collier, 1962.

Crane, Stephen. *Maggie: A Girl of the Streets*. Greenwich: Fawcett Publications, 1963.

-----. *The Red Badge of Courage*. New York: W.W. Norton, 1962.

Crawford, J.P. Wickersham. "The Braggart Soldier and the Rufián in the Spanish Drama of the Sixteenth Century," *Romanic Review*, II (1911), 186-208.

Crofts, J.E.V., ed. *The pleasaunt historie of Lazarillo de Tormes, drawen out of Spanish by David Rowland of Anglesey, 1586*. Oxford: Basil Blackwell, 1924.

Cross, Wilbur L. *Development of the English Novel*. New Haven: Yale University Press, 1900.

Cunliffe, Marcus. *The Literature of the United States*. Baltimore: Penguin Books, 1961.

Daireaux, Max. *Panprama de la Litterature Hispano-Americaine*. Paris: Editions KRA, 1930.

Day, Martin S. *History of English Literature to 1660*. Garden City: Doubleday, 1963.

-----. *History of English Literature 1660-1837*. Garden City: Doubleday, 1963.

-----. *History of English Literature 1837 to the Present*. Garden City: Doubleday, 1963.

Defoe, Daniel. *The Fortunes and Misfortunes of the Famous Moll Flanders*. New York: Holt, Rinehart and Winston, 1961.

Dickens, Charles. *David Copperfield*. 4 vols. New York: Hurd and Houghton, 1863.

-----. *Oliver Twist*. New York: Dodd, Mead, 1941.

-----. *The Posthumous Papers of the Pickwick Club*. New York: Dodd, Mead, 1944.

Digeon, Aurelien. *The Novels of Fielding.* London: George Routledge & Sons, 1925.

Dimsdale, Marcus Southwell. *A History of Latin Literature.* London: D. Appleton, 1915.

Dreiser, Theodore. *An American Tragedy.* New York: Random House, 1925.

----. *The Financier.* New York: Harper & Brothers, 1912.

----. *Sister Carrie.* New York: Random House, 1927.

Duckworth, George E., ed. *The Complete Roman Drama.* New York: Random House, 1942.

Dudley, Ernest. *Picaroon.* Indianapolis: Bobbs-Merril, 1953.

Duff, J. Wight. *A Literary History of Rome.* London: Ernest Benn, 1953.

Elias, Robert H. *Theodore Dreiser: Apostle of Nature.* New York: Alfred A. Knopf, 1949.

Erskine, John. *Galahad: Enough of his Life to Explain His Reputation* Indianapolis: Bobbs-Merrill, 1926.

Fernandez de Lizardi, José Joaquin. *The Itching Parrot.* Trans. by Eugene Pressly, intro. by Katherine Anne Porter. Garden City: Doubleday, Doran, 1942.

----. *Don Catrín de la Fachenda.* Intro. by J.R. Spell. Mexico: Editorial Cultura, 1944.

----. *El Periquillo Sarniento.* Prologue by J.R. Spell. Mexico: Editorial Porrua, S.A., 1963.

Fiedler, Leslie A. *Love and Death in the American Novel.* Cleveland: World Publishing Co., 1960.

Fielding, Henry. *The History of Tom Jones.* New York: Random House, 1950.

----. *The Life of Jonathan Wild, the Great.* London: T. Curson Hansard, 1806.

Flores, Angel, ed. *Great Spanish Stories.* New York: Random House, 1956.

----. *The Literature of Spanish America.* New York: Las Americas Publishing Company, 1966.

Foerster, Norman. *Image of America.* Notre Dame, Ind.: University of Notre Dame Press, 1962.

Ford, Jeremiah D.M., and Ruth Lansing. *Cervantes.* Cambridge, Mass.: Harvard University Press, 1931.

Forster, E.M. *Aspects of the Novel.* New York: Harcourt, Brace & World, 1954.

Forsyth, William. *The Novels and Novelists of the Eighteenth Century.* London: John Murray, 1871.

Friedrich, Werner P. *Outline of Comparative Literature.* Chapel Hill: University of North Carolina Press, 1954.

Gardiner, Harold C., ed. *Fifty Years of the American Novel.* New York: Charles Scribner's Sons, 1952.

Gariano, Carmelo. *El Mundo Poético de Juan Ruiz.* Madrid: Editorial Gredos, 1968.

Gesta Romanorum. Trans. by Charles Swan. London: George Routledge & Sons, 1905.

Gilman, Stephen. *The Art of La Celestina.* Madison: University of Wisconsin Press, 1948.

Gogol, Nikolai. *Dead Souls.* Trans. by George Reavey. New York: Pantheon, 1948.

Gomez, Antonio Enriquez. *El Siglo Pitagórico.* New York: Doubleday, 1962.

Gómez-Gil, Orlando. *Historia Critica de la Literatura Hispano-americana.* New York: Holt, Rinehart and Winston, 1968.

Gonzales-Blanco, Andrés. *História de la Novela en España.* Madrid: Sáenz de Jubera, Hermanos, 1909.

Gordy, Wilbur Fisk. *History of the United States.* New York: Charles Scribner's Sons, 1922.

Grismer, Raymond Leonard. *The Influence of Plautus in Spain Before Lope de Vega* New York: Hispanic Institute in the United States, 1944.

Harss, Luis, and Barbara Dohmann. *Into the Mainstream.* New York: Harper & Row, 1967.

Hawthorne, Nathaniel. *The Complete Short Stories of Nathaniel Hawthorne.* New York: Hanover House, 1959.

Head, Richard. *The English Rogue.* 4 vols. London: Henry Marsh, 1665.

Heller, J.L., and R.L. Grismer. "Seneca in the Celestinesque Novel." *Hispanic Review.* XII, 1944, 29-48.

Hibbard, G.R. *Thomas Nashe.* Cambridge, Mass.: Harvard University Press, 1962.

Hockley, William Browne. *Pandurang Hàrì or Memoirs of a Hindoo.* 2 vols. London: Henry S. King, 1873.

Hoffman, Frederick J. *The Modern Novel in America.* Chicago: Henry Regnery, 1963.

Hogan, Margarita Blondet. "Picaresque Literature in Spanish America." Unpublished dissertation, Columbia University, 1953. (Microfilm).

Hopper, Vincent F. and Bernard S.N. Grebanier. *Essentials of European Literature.* 2 vols. Great Neck, N.Y.: Barrons, 1963.

Howells, William Dean. *My Literary Passions.* New York: Harper & Bros., 1895.

-----. *The Rise of Silas Lapham.* New York: Random House, 1951.

Hunt, Leigh. *Essays of Leigh Hunt.* Ed. by Arthur Symons. London: Walter Scott, 1887.

Jusserand, J.J. *The English Novel in the Time of Shakespeare.* Trans. by Elizabeth Lee. London: T. Fisher Unwin, 1901.

Kettle, Arnold. *An Introduction to the English Novel.* London: Hutchinson, 1959.

Kingsley, Charles. *Alton Locke.* 2 vols. London: Macmillan, 1881.

Kipling, Rudyard. *Kim.* London: Macmillan, 1901.

-----. *Something of Myself.* London: Macmillan, 1937.

Lazarillo de Tormes. Trans. by W.S. Merwin. New York: Doubleday, 1962.

-----. Trans. by Harriet de Onís. Great Neck, N.Y.: Barron's, 1959.

Lever, Charles. *Confessions of Con Cregan.* Boston: Little, Brown, 1904.

Lewisohn, Ludwig. *The Story of American Literature.* New York: Random House, 1932.

Longfellow, Henry Wadsworth. *The Complete Poetical Works.* Boston: Houghton, Mifflin, 1902.

Lovett, Robert Morss and Helen Sard Hughes. *The History of the Novel in England.* Cambridge, Mass.: Houghton, Mifflin, 1932.

MacEoin, Gary. *Cervantes.* Milwaukee: Bruce, 1950.

Manuel, Juan. *Count Lucanor.* Alhambra, Calif.: Carl F. Braun, 1953.

Melville, Herman. *Redburn, His First Voyage.* Boston: St. Botolph Society, 1924.

Mérimée, Ernest. *A History of Spanish Literature.* Trans. by S. Griswold Morley. New York: Holt, 1930.

Morier, James. *The Adventures of Hajji Baba of Ispahan.* New York: Random House, 1937.

Nashe, Thomas. *The Unfortunate Traveller.* Ed. by H.F.B. Brett-Smith. Boston: Houghton, Mifflin, 1920.

Norris, Frank. *McTeague.* New York: Holt, Rinehart and Winston, 1962.

Norris, George Tyler, ed. *Selections from the Picaresque Novel.* Boston: D.C. Heath, 1925.

Oates, Whitney Jennings and Charles Theophilus Murphy eds. *Greek Literature in Translation.* New York: Longmans, Green, 1944.

Pane, Remigio Ugo. *English Translations from the Spanish: 1484-1943* New Brunswick: Rutgers University Press, 1944.

Pattee, Fred Lewis. *The First Century of American Literature.* New York: D. Appleton-Century, 1955.

Peña, Carlos Gonzáles. *History of Mexican Literature.* Trans. by Nance and Dunstan. Dallas: Southern Methodist University Press, 1968.

Petronius Arbiter. *The Satyricon*. Chicago: Pascal Covici, 1927. (Anon. trans.)

Quevedo y Villegas, Franscisco de. *La Historia de la Vida de Buscón llamado Don Pablos*.

Raleigh, Walter. *The English Novel*. New York: Charles Scribner's Sons, 1911.

Real Díaz, José J. "Don Alonso Carrió de la Vandera, autor del 'Lazarillo de ciegos caminantes'," *Biblioteca de Autores Españoles*. CXII, 1959, 245-277.

Rojas, Fernando de. *La Celestina*. Trans. by Lesley Byrd Simpson. Berkeley: University of California Press, 1955.

Ruiz, Juan. *The Book of Good Love*. Trans. by Elisha K. Kane. New York: William Edwin Rudge, 1933.

Saavedra, Miguel de Cervantes. *Novelas Ejemplares*. Trans. by Samuel Putnam. New York: Viking Press, 1950.

-----. *The First Part of the Life and Achievements of the Renowned Don Quijote de la Mancha*. Trans. by Peter Motteux. New York: Random House, 1941.

Salinas, Pedro. *Ensaynos de Literatura Hispánica*. Madrid: Aguilar, 1961.

Salinger, J.D. *The Catcher in The Rye*. Boston: Little, Brown, 1951.

Sands, Donald B. *The History of Reynard, the Fox*. Cambridge, Mass.: Harvard University Press, 1960.

Seidlin, Oskar, ed. *Essays in German and Comparative Literature*. Chapel Hill: University of North Carolina Press, 1961.

Smollett, Tobias. *The Works of Tobias Smollett*. 10 vols. New York: George Routledge & Sons, 1870.

Spectator, The. 8 vols. London: Geo. B. Whittaker, 1827.

Spell, J.R. 'Fernández de Lizardi: The Mexican Feijóo." *Romanic Review*, XVII (1926), 338-348.

-----. "The Genesis of the First Mexican Novel." *Hispania*, XIV (1931), 53-58.

Thackeray, William Makepeace. *Vanity Fair, A Novel Without a Hero*. New York: Random House, 1950.

Ticknor, George. *A History of Spanish Literature*. 3 vols. New York: Harper and Bros., 1849.

Valbuena y Prat, Angel. *La Novela Picaresca Española*. Madrid: Aguilar, 1956.

Van Doren, Carl. *The American Novel 1789-1939*. New York: Macmillan, 1940.

Van Doren, Mark. *Nathaniel Hawthorne*. New York: Viking Press, 1962.

Watt, Ian. *The Rise of the Novel.* Berkeley: University of California Press, 1959.

Webster's New Twentieth Century Dictionary of the English Language, 2nd Edition. Cleveland: World Press, 1962.

Wellek, René and Austin Warren. *Theory of Literature.* New York: Random House, 1949.

Whitman, Cedric H. *Aristophanes and the Comic Hero.* Cambridge, Mass.: Harvard University Press, 1964.

Yearbook of Comparative and General Literature, No. 10. Indianapolis: Indiana University Press, 1961.

Zellers, Guillermo. *La Novela Histórica en España.* New York: Instituto de Los Estados Unidos, 1938.

Index